Leaders to Follow

A Leadership Handbook for the 21ˢᵗ Century

By Jaroslav B. Tusek

with Sara Tusek

International Leadership Institute Publications

Florida and Czech Republic

Publication History: First print edition, 2018

ISBN: 978-0-9786337-6-9

Text and cover design by Noah Shepherd

Published by International Leadership Institute Publications:

21st Century Jobs, Jaroslav B. Tusek and Sara Tusek, International Leadership Institute Publications, Lake Mary, FL, 2nd Edition, 2018.

Prague for Beginners: Finding Myself in Prague, Sara Tusek, International Leadership Institute Publications, Lake Mary, FL, 2017.

21st Century Jobs, Jaroslav B. Tusek and Sara Tusek, International Leadership Institute Publications, Lake Mary, FL, 2009.

Three Things You Can't Do In Prague, Jaroslav B. Tusek and Sara Tusek, Servant Leaders Press (an imprint of International Leadership Institute Publications), Ponte Vedra Beach, FL, 2006.

Your Career Passport, Jaroslav B. Tusek and Sara D. Shepherd (Tusek), International Leadership Institute Publications, Ponte Vedra Beach, FL, 2nd Edition, 1993.

Your Career Passport, Jaroslav B. Tusek and Sara D. Shepherd (Tusek), International Leadership Institute Publications, Sewanee, TN, 1st Edition, 1991.

Leaders to Follow, 1991-2012; *Business Briefs,* 1992-1997.

Careers, 1987-2012; *Servant Leaders,* 2005-2012; *continuous conversion,* 2006-2012.

ALOE: A Lesson on English, 2007-2012.

Other publications:

East Tennessee Business Journal/Chattanooga Business Journal,
contributing editor and columnist, 1993-2008.

College to First Job: Step By Step, Sara D. Shepherd (Tusek), The
University of the South, Sewanee, TN, 1988.

Looking Ahead, Sara D. Shepherd (Tusek), The University of the
South, Sewanee, TN, 1988.

Career Development Handbook, Sara D. Shepherd (Tusek), The
University of the South, Sewanee, TN, 1987.

Designing Your Future, Jaroslav B. Tusek, St. Lawrence University,
Canton, NY, 1985.

*Career Development Kit for Future Leaders: An Introduction to Career
Management,* Jaroslav B. Tusek, American Management Association,
Hamilton, NY, 1984.

*Career Search Kit for International Students: A Handbook of Sources for the
International Job Market,* Jaroslav B. Tusek, New York Institute of
Technology, New York, NY, 1983.

Job Search Kit for the 80s, Jaroslav B. Tusek, New York Institute of
Technology, New York, NY, 1981.

Contents

Foreword: Our experience with leadership development in the *Business Leadership Forum: USA*

If we can't show our kids something edifying, something good and uplifting that we did, something true and honorable to build their souls up and contribute to the common good, then we, as a society and as individuals, have utterly failed. Here is our story of what we've done at the International Leadership Institute to build on the principles and practices of leadership and why we care enough to keep developing and implementing new programs and publications. We've made sure there is something for everyone in this little primer.

Our story

Sara Tusek (ILI Managing Director since 1990 and my wife) and I had the unique opportunity and privilege to participate from the very start in the transition process of the post-communist countries in Central and Eastern Europe (beginning in 1989) as they moved from state-planned economies to fully-functioning marketing economies in the context of newly-built democratic societies. Our *Business Leadership Forum: USA* programs brought hundreds of Central and Eastern European business and government executives to the US for programs to show them one example of a free-market economy operating in a liberal democracy. It was our way of celebrating the "return" and rebuilding of the formerly-communist countries of Central Europe.

As Czech author Milan Kundera put it in *The Tragedy of Central Europe* (1984), the misfortune of post-WWII Central Europe was to be culturally Western, politically in the East, and geographically in the center. The year 1989 could be seen as the reconciliation of culture, politics, and geography, culminating in Central Europe's reclamation of Western identity and conversion to Western-style liberal democracy.

In the hopeful years that followed the collapse of communism in Central and Eastern Europe, it seemed that liberal capitalism and democracy were thriving and that free market economies and human rights would gradually spread around the world, lifting tens of millions of people from poverty, oppression, and a lack of social and economic justice. And it seemed the right answer for the post-communist countries of Central and Eastern Europe to jump on the Western "democratic society" band wagon. This liberal-democratic revolution would restore democratic sovereignty and combine it with the language of civil rights and constitutionalism.

Business Leadership Forum: USA

To this end, we developed and implemented the *Business Leadership Forum: USA* programs, which were designed to help business leaders from Central and Eastern European countries to make a successful transition to open markets operating in democratic political systems and to become increasingly able to compete in the global economy, in spite of their communist past. The *Business Leadership Forum: USA* began in 1991; its programs brought hundreds of Czech and Slovak participants to the US for executive education and leadership development programs that included university seminars, business internships, and (in most cases) home stays with American host families. Later on, we opened the programs to executives from Croatia, Bulgaria, Romania, Macedonia, and several other Eastern and Central European countries.

In order to do so, we used our business, the International Leadership Institute (established in 1985 in Princeton, NJ), to develop strategic partnerships with leading universities and civic organizations in the US and with Czechoslovakia's government, including the Ministry of Industry and Trade. The *Business Leadership Forum: USA* programs operated, with various strategic partnerships, until 2005. Through these programs, we were able to bring groups of 8 to 12 business and government leaders for three-month programs in the US, starting in 1992. Later in the 1990s, these programs were offered for flexible periods of time, anywhere from 10 days to 6 weeks in length, to suit the needs of busy executives as their economies gained momentum.

From 1996—2005, ILI served as a training provider for US AID programs of the US Department of State, Agency for International Development. We custom-tailored *Business Leadership Forum: USA* programs to suit the needs of participants from Macedonia, Lithuania, Bulgaria, Slovakia, Croatia, and Romania.

Because we were directly involved in organizing and implementing all these programs, we were able to observe, from 1991-2005, existing business leadership practices both in the US and Europe and to develop a better understanding of some basic leadership principles that are applicable in any liberal democratic society with a functioning marketing economy. Our programs aimed at the reconciliation of politics, culture, and geography in these countries in Central and Eastern Europe, along with the reclamation of a Western identity—a "return to Europe" and a conversion to political liberalism.

Key lessons and insights

The purpose of this—yet another book on leadership— is to remember some of the important lessons we at the

International Leadership Institute learned as a result of assisting hundreds of government and business leaders from Central and Eastern Europe in their transition from state-planned to free market economies in the 1990s and 2000s. Between 1992 and 2012, ILI published a newsletter, *Leaders to Follow*, which communicated to our stakeholders what was happening with our program participants, their home companies, their US business mentors, their US host families, and all the friends we made in the process. This book incorporates many of the lessons and insights we wrote about in the *Leaders to Follow* newsletter and brings our unique experience into the wider field of leadership education in the 21st century. You can read many of these newsletters at www.ili.cc.

In this book, we provide a summary of seven key principles that can help people prepare for and practice successful leadership in business and in government in the context of a liberal democratic society. By leadership, we mean the ability to influence people to willingly and enthusiastically follow the leader to achieve agreed-upon objectives in any organizational endeavor. We comment on the importance of being sensitive to social and political forces affecting the leader's organization and suggest changes needed as we move forward into the third decade of the 21st century. We offer practical tips for leaders using the seven key principles of leadership which have endured over the decades. The appendices of this book provide comments from ILI program participants and a brief overview of the Institute and our leadership development programs.

Who are we writing for?

As President and CEO of the International Leadership Institute, throughout this book I kept asking myself how I could inject and project the moral and ethical values of my faith into the process of leadership. It is my hope that I have succeeded. The stories, ideas, and advice in this book contain useful and original insights into the social, political, and economic transition process taking place in democratic nations today. Those who choose to apply these insights in their professional and personal lives will benefit in ways that go beyond the traditional idea of leadership roles; the ideas woven into the story offer a perspective that can be helpful today and in the future. This handbook for leaders and those who aspire toward leadership roles (as well as those on whom leadership has been bestowed) is our contribution to the vast topic of leadership. We hope and believe it will contribute to a better understanding and wiser use of the power of leadership.

Preface: Why look at leadership now?

In 1985, about two decades into my professional life, it suddenly dawned on me that, like several of my role models during my graduate school years, I desired to create my own organization which would allow me to be free to do something which I considered important and necessary. This is the genesis of the International Leadership Institute, which has from the start been dedicated to helping individuals develop and use their leadership skills and abilities. My wife Sara became my partner at ILI in 1990 after we'd worked together at St. Lawrence University and found that our professional perspectives complemented each other and added depth to ILI.

After the collapse of communism in Central and Eastern Europe in 1989, ILI suddenly gained the privilege to develop and deliver effective executive education and leadership development programs to several hundred leaders in the post-communist countries. Without working with these leaders, we would never have been able to develop such a unique insight into the leadership crisis in the US of the final years of the second decade of the 21st century: what works and what doesn't work at a time of profound political, economic, and social change in an advanced democratic society.

Leaders are changing, and so is leadership

Sometimes it seems that the only constant thing about the job of a leader in business or government is that it is constantly changing. Right now, leaders are probably spending at least 75% of their time doing things that did not even exist ten years ago.

Accordingly, the concept of leadership is changing, too, in response to dramatic ongoing changes and shifts in both external and organizational environments. Government regulations are changing in both scope and kind; overall economic malaise (beyond anyone's control) and sociopolitical demands are forcing leaders to defend the legitimacy of their government agencies or enterprises. Consumer advocacy groups and other entities are generally critical of business ethics; time spent on litigation is making the legal profession one of the few genuine growth industries.

Changing definitions of equality

In the late second decade of the 21st century, a new phenomenon seems to be emerging. Some call it a leadership revolution, others say it is a new leadership awakening, and yet others define it as a leadership renaissance. Yet another way to describe it is the rediscovery of the key role of leadership in our society. This new interest in leadership is characterized by participation in executive education and leadership development programs, along with soul-searching, self-evaluation, and the conscious realization that, as the saying goes, without vision and without leadership, people perish.

The new breed of leaders interacts very differently with the people they lead than their counterparts did in the 1990s. At that time, leadership principles were based on the perception of equality as a set of conditions that should permit individuals, whatever their origins, to make a life on the basis of ability and character. Accordingly, the idea was that everyone should have an equal place at the starting line and that the definition of the conditions deemed necessary for equality was clear-cut and shared by all.

Major changes in technology, politics, and the economy

Today's leaders have to approach their leadership job with a new perspective that allows them to reflect accurately the ongoing major changes in technology, politics, and the economy, as well as in the larger society and in their business environment. They also must pay attention to significant changes in the values and beliefs that people hold.

Perhaps most importantly, in the 21st century, most people are less willing to accept the impartial operation of "free market" mechanisms as the best way to allocate resources. Accordingly, leaders in advanced democracies have been turning more and more to government to intervene on their behalf. At the same time, the concept of equality has been significantly broadening in the US and elsewhere to include rights to receive a wide range of political, social, and economic benefits; these rights extend not only to traditional privileged groups, but also to women, children, members of minorities, and refugees—the society as a whole.

However, some basic principles practiced throughout the 1990s remain intact, valid, and as solid as ever. In this book we will focus on those enduring key leadership principles that we've identified over the last 33 years as we've run the International Leadership Institute.

Into the future

This book summarizes the results of our observations about general principles and guidelines for effective leadership under any circumstances in an advanced democratic society. We conclude that today's leaders are spending an increasing amount of time on solving problems stemming from external factors and that effective leaders have dramatically changed their basic strategies to deal with social and political forces in the environment. Many leaders now believe that the requirements for a person to be an effective leader today and in the foreseeable future are much broader, more demanding, and more challenging than ever.

Needless to say, these dramatic changes in leadership requirements are altering the internal organizational structure of government agencies and corporations. What are also changing are the leader's relationships with staff, employees, and the executive team, as well as the function of different groups within the organization.

Many people contributed to the experiences discussed in this book. I'd like to thank above all the participants and graduates from ILI programs; the teachers, lecturers, mentors, presenters, and trainers who have generously contributed their time, talent, and enthusiasm; and the ILI staff members and volunteers who've made it all possible. My special thanks go to our strategic partners over the years, both in the US and in Europe; the most significant of these are listed at the end of this book. Above all, I'd like to thank my wife Sara, my partner in business: without her, there would be no book at all.

--Jaroslav B. Tusek, 2018

Winter Springs, FL, USA

Introduction: Leadership principles that endure

Forget the business benefits, the contacts I'm bringing back to my company and all that. Americans here have helped me to push my horizons and change my way of thinking. I'm no longer thinking in terms of lack, loss, and limitation but am thinking more in terms of progress, solutions to problems, and wonderful things which can happen in my company and my country. So be sure to thank all those people who are making this program possible on the American side for what they are doing for us.

–Anna, *Business Leadership Forum: USA graduate*

The International Leadership Institute has made leadership its primary focus since 1985, when it was established in Princeton, NJ. In the past three decades, we have run leadership development programs for Europeans of many ages, backgrounds, and professions, giving us valuable real-life information and experience in helping people develop and use key leadership skills. We have worked with American and European agencies, businesses, and organizations, allowing us to glimpse the inner workings of theses economic and governmental systems.

Visionary leadership that inspires

We find that the topic of leadership is often poorly understood today, leaving people who are moving into leadership roles with no-up-to-date, relevant models. Leadership is often confused with management; leaders are urged to tread softly, in the name of not offending anyone or not being seen as too authoritative, meaning that they may have a diminished impact in the places they are meant to lead.

Too often, organizations "lower the bar" to bring in new leaders (in the name of economy or desperation), placing people with little experience or inclination to lead in positions where they are under intense pressure to lead effectively and efficiently with ever-diminishing resources.

Without such assets as mentors, training, supervision, internships, inspiring examples, and role models, becoming a competent and well-qualified leader is almost impossible. The "trial-and-error" approach of amateur leadership is costly in terms of opportunities lost and mistakes made. In such cases, the leader feels vulnerable, without support, and without a mandate. Such feelings do not build the confidence needed to lead decisively and to inspire those who follow you. Visionary leaders, those who can inspire people to make change happen, have in common several characteristics, skills, traits, and perspectives that contribute to the mastery of leadership; these most crucial qualities are illuminated in this handbook as the seven key principles of leadership.

Our Qualifications

From its founding, the mission of the International Leadership Institute has been to equip executives already in leadership positions, as well as aspiring leaders, with the skills, attitudes, and knowledge needed to succeed in their current or future leadership roles. Our experience of running the International Leadership Institute's *Business Leadership Forum:*

USA in the 1990s and 2000s for leaders from Central and Eastern post-communist countries showed us the complexities of working with a variety of leaders, both cross-generationally and cross-culturally. From our vantage point, we have seen leaders of every description from Europe and the US over the last decades.

Throughout my years of working with and studying under respected leaders from academia, the non-profit world, and business in Prague, Czech Republic; Oslo, Norway; Geneva, Switzerland; Cambridge, England; San Francisco and New York City, USA, I've gained a broad overview of different leadership styles and of leadership role models. During my tenure at the American Management Association in New York, I directed Operation Enterprise programs which were designed to develop leadership skills in young adults, giving me further insight into the mechanics of leadership development. I've used all these experiences and more in designing and delivering executive education and leadership development programs for Americans and Europeans over the past four decades.

Sara Tusek has been the Managing Director of ILI since 1990. In the *Business Leadership Forum: USA* programs, she worked with all our stakeholders including university professors, internship sponsors, seminar presenters, host families, government officials, and participants as she organized, supervised, and evaluated the programs. She produced and distributed all marketing and program materials for the *Business Leadership Forum: USA*; many of her newsletters are available for free on www.ili.cc. In addition, Sara is the Executive Editor of ILIP, the publication arm of the International Leadership Institute. Her talents as an editor and writer include communicating complex ideas in comprehensible ways, making it possible for ILI leadership development programs to help people whose lives and goals are vastly different from each other. She is the author of *Prague for Beginners: Finding Myself in Prague* (2017) and is co-author of *21ˢᵗ Century Jobs* (2009); she plans to publish the updated second edition of *21ˢᵗ Century Jobs* in December 2018.

New pressures on leaders

This leadership primer is also concerned about constraints on leaders due to an expectation that today's leader must make difficult and important decisions with global consequences in a much shorter period of time than was needed in the 20th century. The impact of the global economic competition is relentless.

Leaders now have considerations that were not even on the horizon ten years ago. One very sad and tragic sign of our times that has been in the news recently is that many of the things we buy in our 21st century global economy are produced by people who are working in conditions of slavery. The unregulated slave economy is destroying our environment, wiping out protected species, and contributing significantly to climate change. Honest, dedicated, capable, and well-intentioned leaders are grappling with this tragic situation and are increasingly becoming aware that we need to end slavery around the world. And although slavery may be hidden from public view, these leaders understand that slavers (who don't typically adhere to international laws and treaties) are a leading cause of the natural world's destruction.

The consequences of modern slavery (above and beyond the moral questions it raises) are a growing concern for all responsible leaders, who are judged for their complicity in the slave trade. Leaders have to find time to balance the interests of many constituents in such issues, as they are gaining a greater voice in recent years.

Business Leadership Forum: USA

In a free-market global economy, any company can survive only if it remains competitive. Ever since the collapse of communism in Central and Eastern Europe in 1989 and the early 1990s, hundreds of courageous government and business leaders in post-communist countries have done their part in the process of transferring their dysfunctional state planned economies, plagued by scarcity, bureaucracy and red tape, into fully-functioning, competitive marketing economies. That is what their newly emerging democratic societies required of them. They were determined to put their leadership abilities to the test in their effort to make this rather complex political, social, and economic transition successful.

These were the business and government leaders whom we at the ILI assisted in this endeavor. We did it by organizing executive education programs in the US, designed to help the executives make their organizations competitive. In the process, these executives gained the skills, contacts, attitudes, and knowledge they needed to lead successfully in the global economy.

While these leaders were contemplating the changes their societies needed to make, their US counterparts were already in the early stages of a profound shift from an entrepreneurial economy to the emerging "New Economy" of the then-rapidly-approaching 21st century. As American leaders were trying to live a more holistic life in which education, work, and leisure are in balance (so that they are not victims of building their lives predominantly around work, devoted to one company or an organization), leaders from European countries were coming to participate in the ILI's programs under a different set of circumstances.

A new leadership focus: the greater good

Many of our ILI participants came from European societies that had already found it preferable to focus on broader human welfare, rather than just on personal material advancement, to better respond to the challenges of a world of increasing risk, diversity, and interdependence. They were used to thinking in terms of global consciousness, befitting an increasingly interconnected and inclusive society that is concerned with the greater good. Many of them were multi-lingual and accustomed to adjusting to different cultural norms.

So it seems these executives from a collapsed command economy possibly had some advantages over their American counterparts: free health care, free education, and social benefits such as long paid maternity leaves (up to two years) and long vacations. Their newly-democratized societies emphasized quality of life over the accumulation of wealth; universal human rights and the rights of nature over property rights; community relationships over individual autonomy; and sustainable development over unlimited material growth. And to a large degree, those cultural values have remained intact in the Czech and Slovak Republics (and other post-communist countries) as their economies have grown, demonstrating that ethical leadership is not as impossible as it may seem. As Europeans, these executives preferred the "work to live" way of life as opposed to their American counterparts, who seemed in their eyes to "live to work." We profiled many of these European and American executives in our ILI newsletter *Leaders to Follow,* which we published for more than 20 years; you can read the newsletters for free on our website, www.ili.cc.

The need to be competitive

In the 1990s, the major challenge for these executives was to make their companies competitive again. They came to the US to learn how to implement the knowledge, observations, and useful tips they gained during their stay in the US into their home companies, understanding that no company in a competitive market economy can succeed without having strategies to "make the impossible possible," allowing the company to succeed. Yet while the leaders from post-communist economies were learning how to make their economies competitive, their US counterparts were quietly benefiting from learning through interacting with the European leaders how to make their professional lives more balanced, healthy, and attuned to the coming "New Economy."

It is our hope and positive expectation that those leaders who want to significantly improve their performance, gain some new insights on leadership, and achieve more congruency between their values and the organizations that they lead will find this publication helpful. It is also our hope that a look at leadership in action as shown by today's successful leaders will help aspiring young leaders to gain an introduction into this vital topic. Please consider these chapters as a way to question and dig deeper into the strategies and methods of becoming a successful leader in any endeavor.

Seven key principles for leaders

Principle I: Create unity with a common vision

Pavel, a participant in the Business Leadership Forum: USA, *told us that coming into the program, he felt that he lacked the ability to see beyond the walls of his company. He could not articulate where it was going or how it needed be steered in the future. After completing his program in Florida, he found that the greatest benefit of taking part (aside from improving his skills in the English language) was that he realized the vital importance of having a simple, easily-communicated vision that he could share with the people he was leading. Pavel recognized the need to create unity with a common vision. Clearly, the biggest vision-blinder for any leader is the day-to-day crush of events. Leadership starts with a compelling vision, but communicating that vision on a daily basis is not necessarily easy.*

Making a transition and becoming competitive

Over the years of running ILI's *Business Leadership Forum: USA* programs, we discerned and identified some "secrets" which lead to successful performance and outcomes for those leaders who are willing and able to apply them in their daily responsibilities. These are the seven key leadership principles extracted from running our *Business Leadership Forum: USA* that enabled the participating leaders from post-communist Central and Eastern Europe to facilitate the transition of their economies and companies into the competitive global economy in the 1990s: recapturing their competitive edge, tapping into the global economy, and becoming viable partners for American companies.

Transferring American business techniques and culture to companies in any of the post-communist countries was not without major challenges. What we found possible was to bring together European-style teamwork and cooperation with American-style individualism and stress on competition in such a way that the visiting business executives were able to make their companies competitive again, even after more than forty years of being part of state-planned economies.

The International Leadership Institute (ILI) arose within the global leadership industry early enough to be able to ride the wave of executive education program development. We designed and delivered a variety of professional programs, courses, seminars, and internship experiences as part of the *Business Leadership Forum: USA,* and our programs became a "game-changer" for thousands of business and government leaders from the emerging democracies in the post-communist countries of Central and Eastern Europe. At a time when US companies were at the very top of international executive and leadership education, ILI enabled its US-based program participants to make a significant contribution to the transition of their societies from totalitarian states to liberal democracies with functioning marketing economies.

Entrepreneurial leadership

In the beginning of my experience with the subject of leadership, as Director of Operation Enterprise at the American Management Association in the 1980s, I quickly came to understand that it was increasingly not so much about "becoming a leader" as about being an "entrepreneurial leader" who is visionary as well as transformational. This leader does not just maintain the status quo, but moves the organization into the future.

This idea of entrepreneurial leadership has remained especially attractive to young people, whether we are talking about corporate or social leadership. Yet today's entrepreneurial leaders need to be keenly aware that leadership includes dealing with "followership," for today's leaders are constrained not only by the culture within which they operate but also by their followers, who feel freer than ever to demean, diminish, and debase those at the top. This makes entrepreneurial leaders, as well as all leaders, exceptionally vulnerable to the criticism of those they attempt to lead.

Fortunately, leaders have available helpful tools that enable them to navigate in the rough waters of the global economic environment. There is one tool that is essential and more valuable than any other: the ability to bridge the gap between the widely different ideas and specific urgent priorities of the leader's constituents. Any entrepreneurial leader operating within a free-market economy in a liberal democracy is expected to be able to reconcile these different ideas and competing priorities, so that progress can be made. These leaders must bridge divisive factionalism, both within and outside of their organizations.

The vision that unites

Entrepreneurial leaders are able to influence people to willingly and enthusiastically support and follow the vision and objectives of their organizations. Such leaders create a vision that will unite and mobilize their constituents for pursuing a common vision in the process of fulfilling the agreed-on agenda. The enlightened leader is expected to unify, not to divide and conquer. This means leading one's constituents to become more sensitive to social, political, and global economic factors, to honor the social contract, and to pay attention to all other important factors that influence their organization.

In defining the organizational vision, the crucial criterion is not elegance but sharing a practical and pragmatic motivating idea. The leader has to be able to come up with a simple, understandable vision that will motivate the team to pursue the organizational goals and objectives derived from the vision. The vision needs to be communicated in words so unmistakably clear that the course to the future will be pursued with enthusiasm and vigor.

What is that "master stroke," that simple vision, and how is it developed? It's the leader's responsibility and duty to be constantly on the lookout for external changes that offer new opportunities, even if they may seem initially to be small ones.

It's also the leader's responsibility to imagine what is most likely to happen in the near and the more distant future, and to adjust as well as fine-tune the vision in such a way that it will result in the desired outcomes. The impact of the leader's decisions in that regard is enormous. And if the leader does not take charge of the organization's future, there is no one who will or can—except, and most likely so, the leader's competitors. As Canadian hockey legend Wayne Gretzky put it, "I skate to where the puck is going to be, not where it has been." We'll return to the important role of unity of vision in Principle IV, where we discuss how to develop your full leadership potential.

Setting the course for the future

In fact, this process of being able to envision the results of a decision (factoring in all the unknown and uncontrollable outside influences) requires an astute and creative mind, if not pure genius. In decisions large and small, popular or contested, leaders set the course for their organizations with every move they make. They know that, as a Chinese proverb has it, "you must scale the mountain if you would view the plain."

Most people would collapse under such pressure, but successful leaders rise to the occasion and the challenge to succeed. They rely on the magnetic power of their unifying vision, which is an effective tool to motivate people and to make it possible for leaders to extract sacrifice from their followers and constituents. Such vision can also provide an emotional platform from which to spur followers or workers into being as productive, enthusiastic, creative, and innovative as they can be.

Sharing a unifying vision is a powerful concept indeed, but to develop and share it is a task that is frequently very challenging, exhausting, and time-consuming, if not impossible. The recalcitrant and ever-expanding cast of critical characters who ostensibly constitute the leader's followers and constituents expect that all the most difficult problems connected with the fulfilling of the unifying vision (and the leader's mandate) will sooner, rather than later, be solved by the leader and the team who came up with the vision in the first place.

Not an "impossible task"

Calling the articulation and sharing of a motivating vision an impossible task implies that even the most sympathetic followers are forever complaining or finding fault. Clearly, all leaders need help in developing and pursuing a challenging, unifying vision. Visionary leaders typically appreciate learning the thoughts, ideas, suggestions, and observations of others. They are wise enough to appreciate their followers' attention, advice, and support. But they are also wise enough not to create a platform for enemies to launch their counter-proposals, alternate schemes, and destructive criticism.

Wise, visionary leaders find ways to immunize themselves from negativity and negative thinkers. They keep their vision "sanitized" and "sterilized" by not being unduly disturbed by negative advice and destructive criticism. They listen to compliments and accept them. They listen to constructive criticism and are guided by it. They invite smart people to show them what's wrong with the vision and how it could be fine-tuned to make it work more effectively. And perhaps most importantly, they always continue to press for personal growth and know-how as they see new ways to respond to the vicissitudes of change more effectively.

Take control of your life

These leaders have the courage to say goodbye to the old and obsolete that needs to be buried with dignity before they can say hello to the new, unifying vision that waits with youthful vigor to step in as their new best friend. Such leaders realize that a unifying vision needs to be frequently repeated and followed with some concrete rewards. Former General Electric CEO Jack Welch had a vision to make GE the world's most competitive company. Welch gave our *Business Leadership Forum: USA* participants a copy of his book, *Control Your Destiny or Someone Else Will* and told them, "No vision is worth the paper it's printed on unless it is communicated constantly and reinforced with reward."

Clearly, more than anything else, what a visionary leader needs is the ability to communicate authentically, speaking in ways that ignite people with a vision while carefully listening to what those people have to say. In this way, the wise leader continues to learn each and every day, on the job.

Beginning in the 1990s, we have witnessed explosive growth in leadership and executive education. Partly as a consequence, there has been a silent revolution in recent decades. Effective leaders are using a unifying vision as a tool, partly in consequence of an expanded sense of entitlement—demanding more and giving less—on the part of followers and other leaders' constituents. These leaders have built the expertise to envision possibilities and the power to remain focused in spite of the ongoing changes around them, as well as the ability to visualize and hone their vision. Their ability to persistently communicate an inspiring and uniting vision has significantly contributed to the acquisition of stated corporate goals and objectives. In each culture, there are certain credentials that are fundamental to leadership; communicating clearly is essential in every culture. Amazing things can and do happen when visionary leaders keep their vision and objectives in sight.

Getting personal—questions for your consideration:

1. Why is a unifying vision so important as a tool for visionary leaders and their organizations in today's global economy? Can you give two or three examples of powerful, unifying visions that have worked for you or for others you are familiar with?

2. What do you consider to be the most challenging part of developing an effective vision?

3. What do you stand for as a leader?

    Reflection question: *When so many situations shout for your attention, how can you avoid diversion and stay focused?*

Principle II: Plan, strategize, & communicate effectively

Business Leadership Forum: USA participant Veneta thought that planning is a hangover from totalitarian communism and doesn't amount to a can of beans. During the decades of state-planned economies in the Soviet bloc, those firms and enterprises that were tasked to plan their production and development failed consistently to meet their objectives. Veneta found out during her time in the US that strategic planning (rather than static Five-Year plans that couldn't respond to changing conditions) helps facilitate the desired outcomes of decision-making while fulfilling the organization's vision.

Envision the future

One of the most vital tasks of leaders in fulfilling their leadership roles is to envision the desired outcomes of any decision or policy. This is best achieved through a planning process and articulation of the goals, resources, and strategies of the organization. It all starts with getting excited about the new leadership role, new vision, and new opportunities, and in the process communicating this excitement effectively to all the leader's constituents.

What this thinking process requires above all is profound analysis, creative thinking, and a genuine and in-depth understanding of the assets available, as well as knowing in detail the sources of new information and of their dynamics. Wise leaders chart their course as carefully as captains who look at a map, choose their routes, and calculate the time and resources needed to finish the journey. Such leaders know that doubt finds its life by digging in the cemeteries of dead dreams, but hope finds its life by scanning the horizon for the sunrise coming tomorrow. They cultivate a mental attitude that expects progress in spite of all the possible challenges they are facing, and they never lose their wits in the process. The wisest leaders work well in a collegial environment and have the confidence to persevere in the most seemingly-dire circumstances.

Planning, the new way

Planning (as the term is typically understood) may be incompatible with the emerging economy. Old-fashioned planning can be static and unimaginative, relying on past success and simply trying to project the old ways into an unknown future. No wonder that many see planning as a boring, useless exercise in the repetition of stale ideas.

As many traditional industries continue to decline (along with their outmoded leadership styles and practices), entirely new rules about the value of planning are quickly emerging. The new economy teaches the best leaders how to develop a new mindset, one that is willing to accept higher levels of risk with the hope of higher rewards for the organization in the future. There will always be the risk of failure, but the possibility of success gives these leaders hope and courage.

The new mindset requires leaders to understand that ten years from now, most of their organization's revenue may come from products and services that do not exist today. Most executives do not have a problem with understanding the need for modifications of existing products and services, the immediate value of developing variations of these products, and the expansion of current services into new markets and new end uses.

But to realize that their organization's financial future may depend on entirely new products and ventures that tend to have a long lead time to become profitable takes a truly new mindset, new imagination, and above all a willingness to abandon traditional practices and routines in order to reach out for the right markets with the right products and services.

Strategizing

At the same time, contemporary strategic planning and thinking requires the realization that if today's products and services do not generate a continuing and adequate revenue stream, the company will not be able to make the substantial investment in tomorrow that necessary innovation in the global economy requires. Clearly, the old, reliable planning process has shifted to a new thinking process that requires the leader to become more entrepreneurial, creative, innovative, and committed to excellence than ever before.

It takes maturity and wisdom to pick your battles. There is pressure to continue what seems to be working well and resistance to looking at totally new alternatives. Often, the organization's decision to commit money, time, and talent to a new initiative goes against the desire to keep one's options open, in case something much better comes along.

The new leadership mindset requires above all the willingness to change what's not working any more or what has become obsolete in order to bring new hope and vision in the face of an unpleasant past or present situation. We saw this happening in the International Leadership Institute in the 1990s, when changing circumstances in the economies of the Central and Eastern countries in which we operated caused us to adjust the length, timing, and costs of our *Business Leadership Forum: USA* programs. Each year at our Strategic Planning meeting, we reviewed past programs, publications, and services to better understand what was still relevant and what needed modification or replacement. We kept in close touch with participating government agencies and private businesses, as well as past participants, so that we could accommodate their most significant needs and challenges.

By making these changes, we avoided the temptation to stick to an existing, well-established business model (even if it's not as profitable as it once was), which would have led to a situation in which an organization feeds yesterday and starves tomorrow. This kind of persistence in the face of failing results was an accepted practice in the era of the state-planned economies in most post-communist countries. It is, however, a deadly temptation that has to be resisted at all cost. Waiting until a product or service is truly failing can mean waiting until it's too late to rescue the organization.

Where will the puck be next?

In the 1990s and 2000s, declining companies in Central and Eastern Europe which had been devastated by the state-planned communist era had to innovate and introduce new ways of thinking or find themselves quickly aging, further declining, and then vanishing. Once a company or an industry has started to look back instead of ahead, then it is almost impossible to revitalize it, turn it around, or put it on the path to success, regardless how many great leadership principles the leader will try to use. To use the analogy from ice hockey, executives in organizations and businesses that succeed in the competitive world economy do not focus on where the puck is now, but on where it's going to be. Obviously, these leaders keep themselves informed on current economic and political events around the globe, not just on their own daily concerns. In addition, they have developed the kind of thinking that gives them the capacity for healthy self-criticism so that they can change their strategies rather than clinging to past successes.

Although many of the Central and Eastern European companies our visiting executives came from were suffering from "degenerative diseases" after more than 40 years of communist red tape, bureaucracy, complacency, and a habit of looking back instead of forward, some were able to adapt and survive the abrupt change from being protected by the state to being competitive with every other economy in the world.

Those that survived and even thrived were those that accepted the fact that a radically different leadership mindset can make a difference only if it is complemented by sincere understanding and an eager willingness to innovate and develop an effective strategy that will allow the leader to succeed. The organizations that came through the ordeal of changing so drastically did so by taking severe measures such as breaking huge companies into smaller, more nimble, independent firms that could react to new markets and change products and services to be attractive to potential customers. The non-profitable parts of the company were sold off or shut down; workers either retrained or lost jobs.

Every bit of the old state-run economic security that guaranteed full employment to its citizens was thrown out, leaving many in a state of shock from which they have yet to recover. This has been the steep price of staying in business for many Central and Eastern European companies.

No guarantee against failure

Strategic thinking requires running the risk of failure, a word that many leaders avoid at all costs. But wise leaders realize that there is no shame in trying to do something important and failing. It is much more an embarrassment if the leader is a coward, lacking the courage to try to do something very challenging, important, and worthwhile. The only leaders who never fail are those who never innovate. There are always rewards for trying something new, even if it does not immediately succeed, including the self-esteem generated in honest and noble failure; there are no rewards for those who make a cowardly retreat from great opportunity.

In the kind of innovative and open-minded planning we are discussing, we encourage the consideration of these key strategic principles:

- *Finding and occupying an underserved specialized niche;*
- *Changing the characteristics of a known product, an existing market, or an established industry;*
- *Surprising the customer in a delightful way;*
- *Being first—pioneering new products and services;*
- *Responding to an urgent need or anticipating a need that will surface soon.*

This process of planning and strategizing also requires high concentration, strong focus, and a knowledgeable consideration of alternative ways of reaching the organizational goals and objectives—not necessarily because the new strategies may be less costly or carry less risk but because they may enable the organization to better deal with the competition. The wonderful thing about these strategies is that they are not mutually exclusive, but can be combined in creative ways to match emerging opportunities.

Communicating

While planning and strategizing are critical for leaders who take their job seriously (and ILI programs emphasize the importance of both functions in order to supply the knowledge, skills, strategies, and attitudes necessary in a time of rapid transition to all the participants), perhaps the most important ability for any successful leader is effective communication. Outstanding communication skills are the vital quality necessary for any leader in our multi-cultural global economy.

Discovering what matters is the prerequisite to communicating with a sense of purpose, and empathy (the ability to feel and think as if you were another person) is crucial to good communications. Great leaders can, often unconsciously, discern the motivations and intentions of others. Ignoring (or not cultivating) this kind of discernment frequently results in a pasteurized web of pretense characterized by a lack of specificity and clarity in communicating. This hollow communication style causes followers to lose trust in the sincerity and good will of their leaders. Stemming from this loss of trust comes the inability of the entire organization to successfully compete in the marketplace. The proliferation of new technologies for communicating demands that leaders find ways to be unique in sharing their ideas, feelings, experience, and stories while staying "on message." Enhancing your skills of empathy and conveying your personality in how you communicate is crucial to becoming an effective, persuasive leader who finds ways to inspire those who follow you.

ILI programs have always stressed that leadership is not simply a matter of creating a product or service, selling it, and pocketing the profit, but that all businesses and organizations that are successful over time are built on human relationships. The manufacturing of a product or the delivery of a service, and the marketing and selling of it, are equally important. These are intensely human activities that require well-developed communications skills, and, more often than not, cross-cultural communication skills.

One crucial reason that the leaders participating in our *Business Leadership Forum: USA* programs came to the US (rather than have ILI deliver the programs in Europe) was to gain new insights into prevailing views on a "free market" economy, how it functions in the US, and how the US government enforces the rules and regulations of the game. The goal was not only to learn theoretically how much a government should tax and spend, or regulate, subsidize, and legislate a free-market economy to ensure reciprocity and redistribution vs. focusing on utility and self-interest, but also to see how the US market economy differs from typical European market economies.

Different countries at different times have developed different rules concerning communication based on evolving norms and values in each country. The Central and Eastern European leaders in our programs became aware of the importance of communications during debates over whether the free market is better than government-run economies, who in the US has the most power to make or influence the rules, and whether such rules need to be altered so that more people can benefit from them in the future.

In general, communicating effectively, with all its aspects, implications, tools, techniques, and IT technologies devised over the years, has been leadership's single and most critical challenge. The best leaders are always outstanding communicators; those who communicate poorly (or too infrequently) face a tremendous barrier to being effective leaders.

Vital questions for each leader

- *Am I getting my message across to all of my constituents, not just to my colleagues, employees, board members, customers, and government representatives?*

- *Am I effective in reducing or eliminating misinformation and misunderstanding?*

- *Do I come across as trustworthy, or do I seem to be inept or untruthful?*

While many misunderstandings and misconceptions arise from lack of clarity of organizational goals, policies, and relationships, or the lack of understanding of an urgent need for change, it has been a frequent experience of the executives in our ILI programs that their organizations' structures were so tied up with decades-old red tape, bureaucratic incompetence, and tunnel vision that duplications, omissions, and low productivity defeated efficiency in even the most skillful communications. In other words, even with the best of intentions and a decent level of skill on the part of leaders, communication can be difficult or even non-existent if the company culture is stuck in old, ineffective ways of organizing its memos, press releases, reports, recommendations, and announcements.

However, the best leaders did not allow these problems to defeat them, recognizing that if there is honesty, integrity, decency, and clarity at the highest level of leadership, a respectable level of clarity can be developed at the next level. And if there is substantial understanding at that level, there will be enough of understanding at one level below, too. Any misunderstandings and misconceptions have to be clarified at the top—this is a very important requirement for successful communication. Then the flow of information will be straightforward and believable to everyone involved.

Successful communication tips

If there is any brief recipe for effective communications that we could deduce from our experience gained through ILI programs, it would be this:

- *Clarify the purpose of your communication.*

- *Summarize your main points at the beginning of the communication.*

- *Stick to your subject, resisting the urge to amplify.*

- *Get feedback from the people you communicate with— are you as clear as you think you are?*

- *Keep it simple.*

Whenever effective leaders communicate, they establish a common ground for understanding and for sharing important facts, ideas, attitudes, objectives, and priorities. This common ground prevents duplication of effort, mistakes, incorrect assumptions, and divergent paths of action; it also brings pleasure to routine tasks, as they are elevated in their importance by the tone of such clear and confident communication.

The role of effective communication for leadership is to bridge the gap between the interests and needs of leaders and those of their constituents—employees, customers, distributers, marketers, and company shareholders. The basic principle of communication between leaders and their constituents is tying together their different interests. To this end, leadership books, periodicals, and research papers are full of information about special devices and techniques for effective communications. The latest technologies such as the internet, tablets, smart phones, and new and innovative social media play a large part in the new communications mindset.

Before you decide which technology to use, take the time to review what you really want to say. The effort you put into preparing your message will reap dividends, regardless of the forum you choose. A critical analysis of your message (done before you press the "send" button) can help you avoid using an arrogant or defensive tone. Finding someone who will be honest with you in this analysis is crucial, as we are usually blind to our own faults and weaknesses. You can strengthen your connections to the people you lead by focusing on the clarity, authenticity, and relevance of your communication across the myriad of technologies you embrace. True leadership begins with doing the hard work of creating and communicating your vision with authenticity and trustworthiness.

Everyone has a voice

As instant virtual communication allows everyone to connect with the greater culture and have a voice, we are witnessing the democratization of influence, which means that not only the leaders, the rich, and the powerful have their say. Anyone with an opinion can speak up on the world-wide web and have an influence, giving the average person an ability to effect change to a much larger degree than ever before. This democratization of influence leads to significant changes in the decision-making process laterally, downward, and upward.

This new ability to influence those in power means that the employee may no longer feel at the mercy of some remote, distant "leadership" that controls all aspects of the employee's work. Workers can share ideas, attitudes, and insights through a variety of means, the internet being only the most obvious.

Communication through twittering, chat rooms, instant messaging, social network websites, and text messaging on cell phones or tablets make it easy to keep in constant touch with your peers at work, exchanging information that affects your job and the entire workplace. No longer does information flow down from above in a controlled, orderly manner. Leaders now have to be mindful of and make decisions based on input from those they lead; this is especially central in reacting to situations as they are developing and unfolding. In the process of communicating, successful leaders increase their clarity and deepen their convictions, inspiring everyone involved to move ahead. Without these clear lines of communication, leaders become irrelevant, perceived as passive observers who just let things happen.

Successful leaders make sure that in the midst of this information chaos, they become highly influential and powerful co-creators of reality. They interpret the new reality which is based not only on their plans, strategic thinking, and goals, but also on the input received from all constituents.

And to accomplish that, clearly their ability to communicate in a courteous, timely, appropriate, and tactful manner becomes a highly important skill. All competent leaders demonstrate this skill daily and consistently in their work because they are well aware that the way they communicate is a reflection on their personality, intelligence, level of education, experience, and ability to represent both themselves and their organizations. These successful leaders scrutinize evidence for accuracy before making decisions and statements. They communicate with those whom they respect to gain a different perspective and make sure they are not overlooking a crucial point. These leaders review their own messages for authenticity, reworking when necessary to present their principles, values, and integrity in the communications they approve and distribute.

Politeness, kindness, and courtesy are contagious, and great leaders are the ones who create an epidemic of polite, kind, and courteous behavior throughout their organizations. The ability of leaders to communicate effectively has clear implications not only for the leaders but for their organizations in ways that are not yet fully appreciated and understood; we can say that great communications come from the competence and trustworthiness of the leader who understands both the current situation and the relevant history involved.

Whatever response you, as a leader, want to elicit from your followers must first be present in you. Otherwise, you will be perceived as insincere and false. It's simple courtesy to ask followers to do only that which you, as their leader, are prepared to do.

Getting personal--questions for your consideration:

1. What do you consider to be your major communication challenges in your current leadership role or assignment? Briefly state the challenges and what you are doing to overcome them.

2. Does your former or current organization plan, strategize, and communicate effectively? How would you rate it on a scale 1-10 [1 meaning a lot to be desired, 10 meaning the organization is doing an excellent job in that regard]?

3. Describe briefly the secret of effective communication in your current or former leadership role, using an example of either a notable success or a resounding failure in your communications.

   Reflection question: *Which of the three activities discussed in this chapter—planning, strategizing, or communication—is most crucial for the success of a leader, in your opinion? Back up your choice with an example, either personal or taken from a public leader's track record.*

Principle III: Organize, focus, & prioritize: don't be diverted from your goals and priorities

Business Leadership Forum: USA *participant Zoran was not best known for being an organized and focused person or for having a good balance between personal and professional life. His habits didn't facilitate getting his priorities straight or meeting his goals. He began to see, in the course of his internship, that the best leaders consider life to be too short to waste any time. They take full advantage of their abilities and resources in order to lead effectively. Zoran realized that poor organizational skills cause people to block their own success, and that a lack of focus and ability to prioritize causes people to defeat themselves. He began to cultivate and model the organizational skills he saw in the best executives in his program.*

Keep yourself focused

This may sound like rather elementary advice. Clearly, since childhood most of us have been told again and again that we need to keep ourselves organized and focused in order to do the simplest task. But how many people manage to organize their desk, let alone their work life?

Unless leaders have a thorough knowledge of the economic and technical characteristics of the industry, business, and organization in which they operate, their vital administrative ability and competence as well as credibility will be significantly diminished both inside and outside the organization.

Skillful administration, however, has many dimensions. Consider just three basic competencies:

- *prioritization*
- *handling multiple tasks*
- *processing new information*

Leaders need to cope with many distractions from both external and internal environments including the media, colleagues, social obligations, personal responsibilities, and government regulations. It's easy for them to lose track of what they are already doing in order to deal with a new challenge or new developments. The urgency and importance of a new bit of information, event, or task has to be weighed against the importance of the problem at hand.

Keeping first things first may sound elementary, but it's challenging to do, especially when those around us are pressing us with their urgent needs, desires, and priorities. In particular, the business leader has to be able to recognize the dangers and risks of becoming too involved in the political process. Business leaders may be misquoted or quoted out of context, causing adverse effects in their organizations and discrediting their reputations.

Leaders need to stay informed about the world

One of the most important offices one can ever hold in a free democratic society with a functioning marketing economy is "the office of citizenship." And with this office comes an obligation to be well informed, having a global perspective on both domestic and world events. Today's business, government, education, or non-profit sector leaders have to be sensitive and appropriately responsive not only to what's happening in their home countries but also in other parts of the world.

We have become, whether we like it or not, part of the global economy regardless of where we live and work. That means, in a way, we are in it all together, and whatever major development is happening in another part of the world is likely to have, sooner or later, an impact on our part of the world as well.

The leader has to maintain a careful surveillance of all the forces that impact and influence the organization and discern the key priorities in those areas and among those forces. Clearly, one of the most important requirements for successful leaders is the ability to discern the most urgent and important element among all the things that are coming at them from different corners of their political, social, economic, organizational, and global environments.

Once having set key priorities, the leader must be able to say "no" when necessary without being offensive. Typically, great leaders learn quickly how to delegate work to others without seeming to diminish the importance of the tasks they delegate. This enables them to focus on the most important priority. Leaders must take time to observe, analyze, contemplate, and study issues to be sure they understand all aspects of a given situation. Then is the time for action, which is the most powerful kind of communication.

Once the most compelling tasks are determined and set in order, the leader often works at them simultaneously. Leaders have seldom the luxury of handling just one issue at a time. Because today's leaders operate on much broader canvas than the purely economic, multi-tasking has become one of the essential requirements for most key leadership roles regardless of the type and size of the organization.

The effective leader has to be able to balance constituent interests. Balancing high-pressure multiple tasks may mean putting in longer hours at work but should not lead to an unbalanced, work-dominated lifestyle. Regardless of the number of professional responsibilities that shout for attention, leaders who succeed in the long run learn how to detach from their smart phone at the end of the work day. Exercise, socialization, family time, cultural activities, and travel can be scheduled with the same kind of attention and commitment as work. Recreation (literally, re-creation) boosts energy and creativity, making wise leaders more efficient and productive in their leadership roles.

Processing new information

New scientific, biological, chemical, technological, and other findings are continuously raising difficult and challenging technical questions. They increasingly reflect a growing awareness of modern hazards to human life and the need for national and global policies to reduce these dangers or bring them under control. The ability to smoothly integrate the new data (without getting too upset about them) into existing models becomes a crucial leadership skill.

Just when the leader thinks he or she has everything organized and is ready to start implementing the task with the new facts, an entirely different perspective or information may appear from somewhere. And without a willingness to admit this new information and integrate it within the existing framework, regardless how inconvenient it may be at the moment, the leader is heading for failure. Here the leader's past success in building trust and displaying competence boosts their credibility as any needed changes are incorporated into the organization's response.

All in all, these key abilities of prioritizing, handling multiple tasks, and processing new information into the existing framework differentiate successful leaders from those who are mediocre (or worse). Great leaders realize that the most important resource they possess is not money or profit, but time.

No wonder great leaders take the time to think, to plan, to organize, and to strategize. They are also careful to share this information widely to employees and colleagues so that everyone in the organization can process and assimilate new strategies, ideas, facts, and information. Only by putting effort into such mental tasks can leaders correctly assess where to put their energy, attention, and resources. Again and again leaders fail because they are not willing to "shoot for the moon" and give a new vision the mind-space and time that it requires for development.

Don't be diverted from your primary purpose

Organizing, focusing, and prioritizing energy and attention are all prerequisites for success in leadership roles. Avoiding diversion does not come to most of us naturally. A great leader uses every possible opportunity to be outstanding. Once leaders have established key priorities, they can't give in to anything that gets in the way of the agenda that has been set. Even the leader's other responsibilities or niceties of life can't be allowed to siphon off energy and time that's been already assigned to certain tasks.

Although this may seem rather obvious, it is not always easy to do in daily life. Just imagine the plight of Liljana, a business executive. She's set up her timetable for an important obligation. This means her weeknights and weekends are sometimes used for work. When Liljana's family begins to complain about her being an "absentee member" of the family, letting her know gently that they need her, too, Liljana has to be able to explain diplomatically that, whether she likes it or not, whether she desires it or not, her leadership obligation has to come first (at least for the moment).

Finding the right balance between the personal goals of the leader and the goals of the organization the leader represents is not always easy. It's sometimes challenging to explain to your loved ones that you simply can't be diverted by various exciting and attractive opportunities from your leadership assignment. Your personal, family, social, and recreational life may suffer as a result of your decision to do your job.

The wise leader therefore develops a dual strategy of responsiveness to personal, family, and social responsibilities and to the leadership assignment. The worst possible strategy would be one that is perceived as being not adequately responsive to either one of the two, or to both.

The value of doing what's right

Great leaders gain personal satisfaction from doing the right thing at the right time simply because it is in their "day's work" and is expected of them. Until leaders set aside their own priorities in order to fulfill their leadership role, they have not understood the price of leadership. Needless to say, typically, there is no pat on the back from anyone for doing the right thing. To do the right thing means, above all, to effect change: this is not always appreciated or understood. Yet leaders who can make change happen through the clear articulation and strength of their convictions become indispensable.

Doing the right thing requires leaders to work directly with values and goals so that they can move the organization in a new direction. Such change can be slow, but if it's undergirded with an inspiring and invigorating explanation of the proposed outcomes of the new goal, and supported by the core values of the organization, effective and persuasive leaders can move any organization, regardless of size and slowness to react. They can propel the company or agency in the right direction simply by using the moral and ethical convictions they so eloquently express and by demonstrating how the new goal fits into the historic "soul" of the organization.

These gifted leaders can intervene in the established system and make change happen without firing all the executives or replacing the most experienced employees with cheaper new hires. They don't rely on expensive cutting-edge technology or making new rules and regulations. Instead, these leaders find creative ways to alter the feedback loops, putting in the new goals and technologies in place of the old, tired platitudes.

Rather than pretend to value employees by giving them a tee-shirt, these leaders bring them into the boardroom and listen to their ideas. Rather than rewarding those who never make trouble and follow every procedure unthinkingly, they look for those who have devised new ways to do their jobs more efficiently and productively. The feedback loops are disrupted just enough to allow some fresh air and light into the traditional ways of doing business.

This kind of delicate, deliberate change works for several reasons. First, the leader is seen as a person of integrity and compassion rather than a cold dictator who only wants employees to do things as they have always been done. Second, the leader is constantly seeking feedback and ideas from everyone in the enterprise, not just a few "yes" people in the executive suite. Third, the organization is energized by a current of change in the direction of doing what's right. The people and systems of this revived organization will serve new functions, fall into new configurations, behave in new ways, and produce new results. Naturally, the leader needs to be in close touch with all that's happening in order to encourage what's working well and modify what's not. The best leaders understand the vital importance of lively, relevant communication that clarifies and regulates the information flows.

Effective leaders are also able to deal with both positive and negative outcomes. They do things that are difficult, sometimes unpopular, or downright controversial. They make hard calls and do unpleasant things that must be done. In their own strength, they might not be able to get the job done quickly and efficiently. Therefore they surround themselves with a team of competent and capable people they can rely on. It's the sign of genius in leaders to delegate when needed without giving away so much control that the results are disappointing.

We are now in the middle stages of a major technological transformation which is more sweeping than the most radical "futurologists" yet predict or realize. High tech is now providing increasing numbers of jobs, whether in the form of telecommunications, robots, computers, office automation, biogenetics, or bioengineering, and technology is creating the vision for entrepreneurship and new leadership opportunities. With such exciting opportunities, the ability to skillfully avoid diversion is likely to become increasingly important.

Getting personal--questions for your consideration:

1. Have you ever been in a leadership position in which you had to grapple with finding the right balance between your personal goals and objectives and your organizational tasks and responsibilities? If so, describe in a few paragraphs how you resolved this situation and what it resulted in.

2. This third principle of effective leadership, *be organized and focused: don't be diverted*, requires implicitly that today's leaders are fully committed to their leadership role, are good listeners, honest, trustworthy, encouraging, caring, and able to process new information quickly. How many of these characteristics were you born with? Do you display those traits and characteristics routinely in your current leadership role?

3. Do you tend more often to exhort the strengths and abilities of those you lead in your current leadership role when they are at their best or criticize them when they are at their worst?

4. Do you currently have any particular strategy to make

sure you don't get diverted from your organizational goals and priorities? If so, describe it briefly.

5. Think of times when you performed well in a leadership role by focusing on a specific task or assignment. Now choose three of these experiences to consider, using this model for each experience (Each point should be 3-4 sentences long):

    WHO: Explain who you were leading and why you were involved. Were you asked to lead, or did you take on the leadership role by your own choice? How long did this leadership role last? Were there any problems in leading these people?

    WHAT: Explain what you did, as a leader, using details and specific descriptions. Were you being told how to lead, or did you decide what to do as you went along? Who was supporting you as a leader? Were there any obstacles to accomplishing your leadership objectives?

    WHAT HAPPENED? Consider the results, or outcomes, of your leadership role. Was there any formal evaluation? Did you receive feedback? Can you make any comments about long-term effects on your leadership role?

Reflection question I: Read your three complete experiences. Did any of these leadership roles give you satisfaction? Why or why not?

Reflection question II: Do you currently have any particular strategies to make sure you don't get diverted from your organizational goals and priorities? If so, describe them briefly.

Principle IV: Bring out your full leadership potential & harness it for the greater good

Todor was a Business Leadership Forum: USA *participant who came into the program with the reputation of being honest, trustworthy, a good listener, and encouraging to the people around him. He was bright, imaginative, and able to process new information quickly. Todor seemed to be a "born leader," but somehow he hadn't yet found the perfect fit in his professional career. He hadn't developed or used his full leadership potential. His quest in the program was to find out how to make the leap from middle management to an executive position where he could contribute more of his leadership potential to his organization.*

The need to consider the greater good

The future of companies and organizations is becoming increasingly dependent on leadership's response to the rapidly changing expectations of the general public. Today's leaders find themselves challenged in their leadership roles as they are asked to contribute to the quality of human life. As changing versions of egalitarianism and of social and economic justice are causing "the revolution of rising entitlements" (the term coined by Harvard University professor of philosophy John Rawls), leaders are expected to do much more than just deliver adequate supplies of goods or services.

Now successful leaders also have to set high moral and ethical standards, not only for themselves and their organization but also for their contribution to their communities and the larger society. The general public, mass media, government regulators, competitors, and colleagues are becoming more and more conscious concerning any activity of the leader that falls short of meeting the existing morals, ethical standards, and values of the larger society.

While constraints against dishonest and unethical behavior or practices can be institutionalized up to a point, the leader's work has to be guided by an inspiring example. Setting the right moral tone and consistently providing socially-well-regarded examples of ethical behavior are among the most consequential leadership responsibilities. Failure to do so amounts to dereliction of duty. A leader's reputation, or "credit rating," is crucial to his or her ability to gain and keep the trust of followers.

Because of ongoing major changes taking place in both the internal and external environments of any organization, it is important for leaders to channel their qualities and abilities for the greater common good and keep looking at their organizations from the viewpoint of the larger society. Each leader has to be well armed with accurate (not misleading) information about the social, economic, and political aspects of the issues that he or she chooses to address. This involves sifting out the good and constructive from the bad and destructive.

Leaders cannot be afraid to install an inner censor to stand at the portals of their minds, checking the ethical and moral credentials of ideas that could disrupt, disturb, subvert, corrupt, and possibly destroy their positive attitude along with their sense of moral responsibility.

Reputation is instant, for good or for bad

One of the effective leader's priorities must be to help develop the organization's public affairs program to deal with issues such as the building of constituencies to support the organization's position. Failure to do so would almost certainly result in further eroding of the already declining credibility (in the general public's mind) of today's leaders for doing the right thing.

Perhaps nothing is more important for leaders than to believe in what they are doing and to know who they are. Leaders often overlook their own very best qualities and don't realize how unique they are or how extensive is their potential. Typically, they remain unaware of the range of their capabilities and deny the possibility that they, too, can aspire to goals previously beyond their reach.

It's crucial that all those who lead have a firm grasp on the strengths, weaknesses, and unique qualities in their possession in order to have confidence in their abilities and not feel overwhelmed by the constant challenges they face, while avoiding the arrogance that comes with not knowing when and who to ask for help when necessary. Authenticity is paramount. Connecting with others is, to a large degree, dependent on the leader's choice to be genuine and approachable.

Most importantly, leaders have to be thankful for and pay special attention to their advisers, counselors, and supporters. These very valuable people not only encourage but also inspire leaders to develop their potential. A positive and productive approach to the leader's work and life consists of appreciating and hearing the thoughts, criticism, concerns, ideas, and observations of others, especially those who matter most: the public, customers, clients, competitors, co-workers, government regulators, employees, trustees, stock owners, and world leaders of successful advanced democracies.

Those who lead have to be aware that the power, authority, and influence of all those constituents is growing, meaning that leaders have less authority to make unilateral decisions and to ignore the repercussions of the policies they enact.

Social issues are not to be ignored

Today's leaders operate on a much broader canvas than the purely economic or political one. The more they are concerned about their responsibilities toward larger society and general public, the more they can reflect the ongoing changes in the workplace, such as the decline of the traditional working class. The broad demand for an improved quality of life and health has been translated into specific public cries for everything from pollution-free working and living environments to materially improved quality and longevity in products and services.

Those leaders who are not prepared or poised to address such issues will fall behind, becoming significantly weakened leaders with many alienated constituents and followers. Increasingly, leaders need to be sensitive to the people around them. Intimidation and lack of concern for others' feelings may seem to work as a strategy to accomplish certain tasks but cannot build the kind of real and robust contributions needed for an organization to thrive and innovate.

Without a public perception that the business, corporation, or organization is sensitive to and reacts appropriately to social and public concerns, and without a legitimate involvement in the social arena to contribute to the greater common good, it's difficult to imagine any substantial increase in the credibility and sustainability of an organization. A lack of proper engagement in the public arena would result in continual eroding of public trust in all major institutions of a liberal democracy, which will impair the ability of any leader, in any arena, to lead with confidence.

Clearly, entering the third decade of the 21st century, leadership is considerably different from the 1990s and 2000s: more challenging and more difficult to exercise, more influenced by public demands, and necessarily more engaged in the political, social, and economic spheres.

Tyrannical leaders (in business and in politics) who refuse to change in view of these developments are by and large doomed, while political leaders in democracies are more and more constrained by the ideologies that underpin a free, functioning democracy, and also by structural strings that include institutional checks and balances. This constraint comes through technologies that enable and continue to expand dissemination of information and freedom of expression, as well as through followers feeling more important, entitled, and emboldened.

A move away from authoritarianism

What this means is that the new leaders who are keeping up with developments that spread power more evenly across the society can't model themselves on the old autocratic models of authoritarian leaders who command and expect obedience. Modern followers in advanced liberal democracies have too much access to valuable information to be bullied into compliance. At the same time, relatively free access to information means that leaders who try to honor the traditional processes of democracy that limit power in ways that are meant to promote social justice will find themselves undercut by constituents who know as much as the leaders do (if not more) about issues that affect them.

When voices from both inside and outside of organizations and in the larger society become louder and harsher and carry much further, leaders have to change whether they like it or not. The most successful leaders don't ignore these voices—they listen, and they change. They don't wait for problems to become insurmountable; instead, they are proactive.

These wise leaders assemble a team of colleagues, co-workers, and employees who are actively thinking about the vision and mission of the organization. This team works for the greater good, looking at what is working well and what needs to be modified, overhauled, or scrapped altogether. In the process, the team discovers new opportunities that the organization can pursue.

Nothing is more important for today's leaders than to earn the respect of all their constituents by sincerely practicing mutual trust and teamwork. By bringing together all the people who are affected by the business, agency, or institution that they lead, wise leaders earn the genuine power needed to steer their organization in times of tremendous change.

Imagine the outcomes of your decisions and policies

Leaders, like everybody else, often overlook their very best and most important qualities for their leadership role by taking them for granted. They remain unaware of their capabilities and of the importance of their imagination and enthusiasm for achieving their goals and objectives.

In the 1980s and 1990s, American business leaders had a love affair with the idea of "vision." Vision was a tool to motivate people to do everything they could to achieve all they were capable of achieving. At the same time, vision also made it possible for business leaders to extract sacrifices from employees. Vision provided an emotional platform from which to spur workers into being as productive as they could be in light of budget cuts and downsizing.

As a concept, vision was successful, as the high levels of American productivity (even in the face of a steady loss of real wages) demonstrate. The organization's vision was a powerful tool for leaders to vocalize their thoughts, provide positive reinforcement for organizational goals, and inspire all those who wanted to be on board with them to achieve the desired results.

Through the process of visualization, the leader's constituents used their imagination to see what they were being asked to accomplish together. Once such creative thoughts were established, the leader could assist his or her followers to transform them into reality. But vision had to be far more than just a fad or a corporate mantra. It had to really inspire and motivate people to achieve common goals. For most businesses, vision had to clearly and very succinctly communicate a program of ideas to provide products or services that solve problems no one else was really tackling. This was the only way for vision to inspire innovation and creativity, as leaders in the 1990s discovered.

Visions that motivate

A motivational vision has to be complemented by a personal positive attitude. Each high-achieving leader has to be able to imagine the constructive possibilities and outcomes which will actually transpire as a result of his or her creative imaging. Once the leader has firmly established the vision, it can be used to unite and motivate the organization as a whole. But whether or not this happens depends on the leader's ability to mobilize the leadership team to include the use of creative visualization.

As members of the leadership team begin to determine what they actually want to accomplish, they need to agree on the rough likeness, image, or symbol of their ultimate intent. With enough interest, imagination, and common purpose, they will be able to more clearly discern their ambition. It's essential for the leader and the leadership team to visualize all the possible results before they decide on their action plans.

In the process of imagining the results they wish to achieve, they have begun to make the chosen outcome into reality. Visualizing a goal in this way enables them to obtain it. What people see and feel in one dimension can be translated to others through imagination and skill at sharing their vision.

How did Beethoven triumph over deafness to compose majestic music? How did Milton defeat blindness to write words of depth, magical power, and beauty? How did Helen Keller, who could neither see, hear, nor speak, achieve more than most people can imagine? How did William Blake capture the image of something as vast as eternity in his inspiring words, "To see a universe in a grain of sand and eternity in an hour"?

These people and many others who became prominent leaders in their fields of endeavor define not only the essence of courage, determination, self-knowledge, commitment, caring, strength, and perseverance. They also demonstrate the power of creative visualizing. Most of all, these high-achieving people found ways to bring out all of their human potential and harness it for the greater good. They communicated authentically, on the basis of their true values, using the raw material of their own convictions. They were aware of and responded to their calling to express themselves where they could best contribute their entire personhood.

Getting personal--questions for your consideration:

1. How have the changes in technology, access to information, and education forced leaders to become more attuned to issues outside of their own business or organization?

2. Leaders who don't assume broader leadership responsibilities to the general public and the society at large are perceived by many as ineffective and weak. How can they convey their values and commitment to these broader responsibilities?

3. Should leaders be concerned with social, political, economic, and environmental changes in areas that don't directly touch on their companies or organizations? Briefly discuss your opinion, giving an example of a leader you can admire in this regard.

   Reflection question: Give just two or three examples of the major changes you have been experiencing in your current leadership role. How are you managing the stress and using your leadership potential to its maximum potential?

Principle V: Do not underestimate the importance of building coalitions & strategic partnerships

Ivana was an outstanding chess player with the ability to look at the board and imagine how the pieces could be moved to assure her victory. In her Business Leadership Forum: USA *program, her habit of considering how each move influences the outcome was a notable asset. In addition, Ivana had the reputation of being skilled in working with a team, yet she hadn't moved beyond the small team of close associates whom she'd worked with for years.*

This team had been successful in terms of what her organization had already achieved, as they had a deep understanding of its abilities and strengths, but they were at a standstill when considering initiatives and new projects that went beyond what had been done in the past. Ivana had powerful skills of imagination and analysis that could be applied to the future of her organization, but she was missing a crucial component—a team that could take everything to the next level. She began to see that short-term strategic partnerships assembled for specific projects could add innovation and a fresh perspective to the organization's vision and mission, and she could observe how strategic partnerships actually worked in her Business Leadership Forum: USA *program.*

Imagining the outcomes of your decisions

As a result of today's economy becoming ever more complex and competitive, organizations and businesses have been moving from a time of intense competition and selfish self-reliance (a "dog-eat-dog, prepare-for-a-shark-attack, or use-guerrilla-warfare-tactics" world) to a new era of cooperation, interdependence, and teaming up with strategic partners.

The leader's ability to envision new possibilities and develop a unifying vision now often includes a vision of collaborating or teaming up with other organizations in order to further the leader's strategic goals. Making strategic partnerships can help the leader leverage organizational resources as well as to keep up with (or ahead of) competitors. Strategic alliances have the potential to reduce risks, increase success, and grow a business.

ILI's strategic partnerships: the only way to go

When we launched the International Leadership Institute's executive education and leadership development programs, in the early 1990s, we partnered with several universities, a number of Chambers of Commerce (both in the US and in Europe), hundreds of American businesses and corporations, the Czechoslovak Ministry of Industry and Trade, and the Olomouc Training Center in the Czech Republic, among others.

We knew that our ability to deliver our very ambitious programs was going to call for a new way of working, using a variety of collaborative and innovative methods. Our need for strategic partnerships arose from a desire to expand our programs to reach as many participants as possible and to win their respect by working from a position of strength and competence.

We also knew that without such strategic partners, we would not have enough staffing, credibility, and financial resources to deliver programs of high respectability, lasting quality, and meaningful impact. Our entering into a broad spectrum of mutually beneficial relationships enabled us to accomplish our goals and objectives while also solving legal, financial, staffing, and other issues.

In the process, we discovered that cooperation and interdependence enabled us all, including our participants, to gain substantially more than we at ILI would have found possible working solo.

Moving from self-reliance to cooperation and interdependence with our strategic partners enabled us at ILI to create expanding possibilities for executive education and leadership development programs.

These programs met the specific conditions and needs of the executive participants from the post-communist countries of Central and Eastern Europe with which we worked. The strategic partnerships we established proved to be ideally suited for working with the developing marketing economies of Central and Eastern Europe, as well as for operating within the emerging US economy of the 1990s. Clearly, establishing strategic partnerships was a new, better, and different way of doing business.

However, we were also aware that to gain support for a needed change in doing business, it was essential that we create an environment in which people could feel safe to honestly express real thoughts and feelings, including disagreement. We knew we must learn quickly how to interact consistently in a way that engendered trust and inspired commitment from our colleagues and partners. Without empathy for others, the entire endeavor of establishing strategic partnerships would most likely fail; shared responsibilities would be misunderstood and could not have produced the desired results.

The possible downside of sharing of responsibilities was a relatively small price to pay when we consider our initial mixed feelings about getting involved professionally and financially with someone else. While some visionary and entrepreneurial leaders may have reservations about teaming up with other organizations because they are independent-minded and self-directed by nature (and are used to calling the shots and being in charge of their own fate), there are too many major advantages and benefits stemming from teaming up to ignore the upside of making strategic partnerships.

The new normal: teams for specific purposes

Teaming up with other organizations is becoming a modus operandi for many businesses and organizations—a new paradigm for survival and success in the global market place. When teaming up works well, no one gets taken advantage of, and no one gets the short end of the stick. Each party brings something special and valuable to the table. To ensure this kind of outcome, leaders must have powerful skills of negotiation and enough in common to hear each other's ideas and needs correctly. Cooperation, teamwork, and mutual benefit reigns supreme. There are so many advantages and rewards of this cooperative approach to work and reasons for seeking strategic partners that teaming up is becoming more and more popular for both big and small organizations.

It seems obvious that successful strategic partnerships require all those involved to have well-developed negotiating skills, a great deal of well-earned trust in one another, and a good measure of vigilance, because even the most well-meaning partner can inadvertently lead others down an unwanted path. One should not overlook the reality that people don't always do what you expect them to do, which is the one thing that most often leads a strategic partnership astray.

Needless to say, building strategic alliances and partnerships will never be a guaranteed route to personal, economic, and financial survival. There will most likely be misunderstandings and difficulties in getting along among the partners.

Taking the time to look into a person's or company's background and suitability for strategic partnership is required for your own protection. Doing a thorough check includes getting a sense of the person's previous track record, financial background, and work quality. Whatever has steered a leader to consider teaming up with someone, it would be unwise to proceed without doing "due diligence," whether it is done through formal or informal techniques like discussing with the potential partners the kind of projects and work they've done in the past.

When to look for partners

Notwithstanding such concerns about suitability and reliability, there are many situations in which alliances can be very valuable for many organizations. Here are some reasons for forming strategic partnerships:

1. Joint efforts among different organizations can make it easier to quickly find necessary resources and to solve common problems with health and disability insurance policies, credit lines, tax laws, funding, and other crucial matters that saddle a single organization with heavy burdens and place limitations on it.

2. Often a single organization simply does not have the time, staffing, expertise, money, or know-how to meet all the challenges of an interesting project, or to make most of the opportunities the project or the task ahead of them provides. While leaders may not be able to rapidly grow their organizations alone, with appropriate strategic

partners the organization's operations and outreach can expand without expanding its costs and overhead.

3. Teaming up often leads to enhancing the credibility and reputation of an organization and its projects, product, or services. As a result of a successful strategic partnership, services or products offered are taken much more seriously.

4. Partnerships enable organizations to avoid professional isolation and instead gain vital inside information about their industry.

5. Operating with adequate strategic support systems to spur growth may help to discourage competitors from trying to offer similar products or services because of the complexity of the issues involved.

6. The urgent need to find creative solutions to make the most of new or existing opportunities within the options open to a single organization, combined with the desire to generate more business, often leads to the willingness of a leader to lose a little bit of the organization's independence by seeking reliable strategic partners.

More pros than cons

To sum up, teaming up enables leaders to both seize the opportunities and overcome the challenges of being their own boss. It also enables them to create and share a multitude of new "pies" rather than just fighting over a limited number of existing ones. It's the best way for any organization to make sure it is being taken seriously. Strategic partnerships provide both small and large organizations an opportunity to test their new business ideas with less risk and more impact. By teaming up, organizations can gain access to new clients and new markets, can make contacts more readily in other geographical locations, and can share expenses to stretch a tight budget.

Perhaps the most important single factor spurring so many organizations to link up with others in new ways is the relentless shrinking of the corporate workforce that has been occurring over the last several decades. As tens of thousands of large organizations and corporations are being forced to cut costs by reinventing and reengineering themselves to better fit into a new information and service global economy, they are emerging leaner, trimmer, and meaner. With fewer employees to work on new projects, teaming up with other organizations makes more sense than ever before.

When we started our *Business Leadership Forum: USA* programs at the International Leadership Institute in the early 1990s, we were at first not taken very seriously by all of the leaders we wanted to reach. But the moment we teamed up with several government agencies, universities, major corporations, and non-profit organizations, our luck changed considerably. Not only did our programs gain a much higher status, but as a result we could expand, improve, and offer them to more government and business leaders than we ever dreamed of.

This enhancement of our reputation led to our being offered the opportunity to run custom-tailored leadership development programs in Bulgaria, Macedonia, Croatia, Lithuania, and Romania for the US Department of State Agency for International Development. Our strategic partnerships were vital in delivering the *Business Leadership Forum: USA* programs, and we owe much of the success of these programs to these universities, civic organizations, and businesses. In Appendix III, we list of some of our most important strategic partners.

Getting personal: Questions for your consideration:

1. What are some major reasons for teaming up with other organizations that make the most sense to you and to your organization?

2. If you have already been a strategic partner for a while and find yourself now disagreeing with another or more of your partners, what can you do to solve the problem?

3. What do you think you need to aim for when you are creating a new strategic partnership?

4. What can you do when strategic partnerships go sour? How can the inevitable disagreements be settled in ways that the partnership can go forward?

Reflection question I: *What are two or three objections that come to mind at the prospect of working with other organizations?*

Reflection question II: *What could you do to avoid the consequences of a partnership in which competing interests threaten the ability of the partnership to continue?*

Principle VI: Use your power in ethical ways

Boris was used to one way of doing things in business: using intimidation to get people to submit to his requirements. His experience in his home country as a restaurant inspector during the totalitarian rule of communism gave him plenty of opportunities to use threats to make managers comply with his "recommendations." He didn't always enjoy playing the bully, but he knew no other way to get results quickly. When communism toppled and the old power structures collapsed, Boris lost his state-supported source of political power. He was adrift, having never developed his own understanding of morally and ethically acceptable ways to use power. He needed to learn how to use power not for personal gain but for the good of the organization and the society in which he lives. The Business

Leadership Forum: USA *introduced Boris to leaders who were adept and skilled at using power in ways that upheld their own ethics and social values based on democracy, respect for the individual, and the idea of working for the common good.*

The interaction of power and ethics

In the previous five principles, we focused on our daily encounters with the participants in the *Business Leadership Forum: USA* programs that took place in the 1990s and first years of the 2000s, the new millennium. These five principles delineated how leaders can react in effective ways to ongoing changes in their own countries and the rest of the world. Our emphasis in those years was on helping leaders who were coming out of totalitarianism into free markets and liberal democracy, and we stressed the techniques and strategies needed to make the leap from state-planned to competitive, open economies. These leaders and their organizations were in the midst of transition, and old habits die hard; we offered new ways of thinking and doing to replace those habits.

While the five principles have enduring relevance and significance for leaders today, they are not enough. In the years since we were immersed in the *Business Leadership Forum: USA*, the world has been changing perhaps more rapidly than ever. As power has shifted among nations and new political philosophies have grown, we are observing dramatic alterations in the tasks and priorities of leaders.

Gone are the taken-for-granted certainties of the Cold War era, where agreed-on ethical and moral stances were associated with particular ways of running a government and an economy. There are hundreds of political analyses and opinion pieces that attempt to document the reasons for this shift; from our perspective, the "why" is not as important as the fact that no longer can leaders assume that their counterparts share their core beliefs and ethical framework.

This is, we think, the most crucial challenge for leaders as we near the third decade of the 21st century: to carve out their own belief system based on decency and taking responsibility for their actions. This is especially true in countries where the highest level of leadership appears to have departed from working for the common good, where divisiveness gives rise to inequality, and where the average citizen cannot depend on leaders to use their power in ethical ways.

Considering the importance of using power in ways that are ethical is not just about what is legal or illegal. Rather, ethics involves questions that seek to discover what is right versus what is wrong. Ethical considerations give preference to principles about what is decent, honorable, and most beneficial for all parties involved rather than giving preference to standards that give leaders unlimited power to make and enforce decisions.

Although this may seem like a simple statement, it's actually a revolutionary way to approach the interaction of power and ethics. This interaction becomes especially evident when the ideas and initiatives we value deeply are questioned or challenged.

For most people, the very definition of power is the ability for leaders to make decisions and take actions that benefit themselves. Why would anyone suggest that this is not right? And why bring ethics, a complex set of values and beliefs that are usually seen as connected to specific cultures, into the picture at all? Surely ethics are for university professors and people in religious orders. No one expects the average person, let alone powerful leaders, to place the needs of others on a par with their own. There are exceptions: politically-aware young people, as we can see in the news, are redefining power, and some well-known idealistic leaders have shown us that it's not impossible to use power responsibly. But for the most part, we don't have many inspiring role models for morally-acceptable behavior by current leaders.

However, the fact is that, in a world where technology connects everyone instantly and relentlessly, it's not possible to ignore the ethical dimension of leadership. As humans move away from authoritarian leadership (dictatorships, "strong-man" governments, top-down decision-making, and the traditional hierarchies that favor certain types of people over others) towards more collaborative leadership (democracies, communities, and social groups based on shared goals, commonly-held principles, and consensus, as well as groups that come together for specific purposes and then disperse), leaders are vulnerable in ways they don't always anticipate. Their power must be used more adroitly than in centuries past, as their actions are scrutinized by the entire world. Empathy is necessary for leadership, and successful leaders are expected to be sensitive to the cues of those around them. This expectation is becoming more and more evident as we live in an increasingly interdependent world.

Treat people with respect and decency

One universal ethical standard can be summed up this way: treat people, all people, decently. Within that standard are several variables, including the definition of decency. Some leaders can and do manipulate these definitions to justify or soften their actions, but only the most eye-blinkered followers will be fooled. For the leaders who want to act with integrity, who are serious about using their power ethically, this standard is surprisingly useful and comprehensive.

First, who are "all people"? Customers, employees, stockholders, professional colleagues, and the general public all fall into this category. Leaders who strive to make ethically-defensible policies and actions will need to consider each of these constituencies each time they make a decision.

This can be exhausting and time-consuming, so often leaders are tempted to take short-cuts when overwhelmed by the need to act quickly and decisively. Their excuse is the urgency of the situation.

One practical way to deal with this threat to ethical decision-making is for leaders to set up ways of constantly monitoring the changing perspectives of the people with whom they interact. Governments do this when they create bureaucracies: the Department of State for foreign affairs, the Department of Labor for regulating the job market, and so on. Every leader can do this in a more straightforward way by simply meeting periodically with all the groups he or she affects. Sharing a meal, visiting people where they live and work, sending e-mails and short videos: all these rather obvious means of keeping relationships alive will work for the leader who is determined to know enough about "all the people" to figure out how best to meet their needs and consider their interests.

Decent treatment includes respect for a person's ideas, beliefs, heritage, opinions, and perspective. To take this idea further, respect must include a sincere desire to help people grow and develop, an aspiration to lift people up rather than smash them down, and a commitment to allowing people to maintain their privacy. Now it becomes evident that ethical leaders have a huge task in understanding the people that their decisions affect; only constant intellectual, spiritual, and emotional growth and exploration can lead to this kind of profound understanding. Our *Business Leadership Forum: USA* programs provided ample opportunity for participants to evaluate their own level of personal moral development and find role models to inspire them with fresh insights into operating in ethically-responsible ways.

Of course, we encountered *Business Leadership Forum: USA* program participants whose behavior was questionable, problematic, and not based on morally and ethically acceptable behavior. Many of these came through our earliest programs, when we had some participants who were determined to adhere to the methods and thinking of the old, out-of-power totalitarian regimes in which they first gained power. Such participants required our special attention and a great deal of our time; in a handful of cases, where their behavior was disruptive to the other participants or their host families, we had to ask them to leave their program and return home.

Clearly, our programs emphasized what we considered to be widely-held definitions of ethics (in relation to power) that were basically the same in any functioning free-market economy operating in a liberal democracy. We were of the opinion that good relationships are built on trust and shared values rather than on coercion or bribery, and we insisted that the basic principles of mutually-beneficial interactions (including decency and ethical uses of power) would be practiced in our programs, to the best of our participants' abilities.

Clarifying values and standards

As we see it, the ethical leader cannot automatically choose financial gain (profit) when making decisions. This statement may seem counter-intuitive, especially in business when top leaders are chosen with the hope that they will increase profitability and cut costs. Yet an ethical leader can successfully operate within these constraints by clarifying the values and standards in such a way that people are treated decently. Here are a few ideas for doing so:

1. Keep the horizon of achievement as far in the future as possible. If the measure of success is the current quarter, it's difficult to decide what to cut or what to keep when profits are declining. By placing markers that continue for years (quarterly, annually, the next five years, the next ten years), the leader can strategize over the long haul. One quarter's poor performance is balanced over the course of a year or more.

2. Make a policy of putting people first. For any organization, salaries and benefits typically account for 60-80% of expenses. It's very tempting to freeze or lower salaries, cut employees' hours or benefits, lay people off or fire them, or choose not to hire new people when employees leave, spreading their work among other employees without compensating them for their new responsibilities. In fact, these strategies are commonly taught in business schools. But some organizations make a pledge to their employees to treat them decently, just because it's the right thing to do.

3. Keep close tabs on what is working and what is not, and adjust accordingly. In any organization, there's a natural tendency to hide failure. The best leaders find ways to track performance without making employees feel oppressed or spied upon by making it part of their daily routine to communicate with all the people for whom they make decisions. Of course, cynics will see this as a ploy to find the problems and fire the people held responsible, but ethical leaders will persevere in the face of such criticism. Only by knowing what is actually going on in their organization can leaders use their power ethically.

By now, you can see that the simple statement, "treat people, all people, decently," is far from simple. It requires that leaders turn themselves inside-out, examining their own motives and questioning their own decisions. Leaders need to have a firm knowledge of what they consider right and wrong; they need to put people ahead of profit; they must choose the hard path of not putting their own self-interest (or that of their organization, at times) ahead of all else.

How power changes the brain

The power of leadership does not come without a price. It's commonly accepted that people who gain and use power often have a greater-than-normal challenge when it comes to ethical decisions. "Power corrupts," people say, with resignation in their voices. It's just part of the package that the acquisition of power tends to produce ethical weakness.

What happens to people when they become leaders that makes it so difficult to act ethically? One intriguing area of scientific research makes the suggestion that power causes actual physical changes in the brains of people who exercise power. This might seem impossible to prove, since power is not easily observed, let alone quantified or measured, in the same way that one can detect the presence of neurotransmitters or neurons in the brain. But surely the ill effects of power are well-known: euphoria, intoxication, and a sense of self that is out of proportion are all states of mind that power produces. Could it be that these emotional states (especially when experienced over long periods of time) change the chemistry of the brain?

Studies indicate that people with high levels of access to power do change. They become less aware of risk (and more reckless), more impulsive, and less able to see things from another person's perspective. Their levels of compassion and empathy diminish as their sense of personal supremacy increases. While their leadership performance may remain acceptable, especially if they have good institutional support, their tactics and techniques may show a tendency toward cajoling, applying pressure, and bullying to get their way. They are so sure that their way is best that they sometimes lose sight of the ethical consequences of their decisions. Without facing their own failures and recognizing their own dark side, such leaders are unable to move beyond narcissism, narrow self-interest, and "group-think" strategies.

Lord David Owen, British neurologist turned parliamentarian who also served as British Foreign Secretary, is the author of "Hubris syndrome: An acquired personality disorder? A study of US Presidents and UK Prime Ministers over the last 100 years," an investigation into physical maladies that affected the performance of British prime ministers and American presidents since 1900. Together with

Jonathan Davidson, Lord Owen conducted a study concerning a "disorder of the possession of power." This study established fourteen clinical features of the "hubris syndrome" of leadership, including "manifest contempt for others, loss of contact with reality, restless or reckless actions, and displays of incompetence." Could it be that leaders develop psychological disorders that cause them to screen out peripheral information that does not agree with their preconceptions, thus making such leaders obtuse?

What are the ethics you live by?

This is where ethics come into play. The best and brightest leaders realize that acting according to a set of humane ethics can produce good results. Focusing on the demands of conscience, fairness, compassion, decency, honor, and respect for others can help leaders avoid the pitfalls of power. Ethical principles, when heeded, lead to ethically-responsible behavior; the lure of the hubris syndrome can be withstood if leaders stick to the ethics they have defined for themselves. Finding like-minded people (even those not in leadership roles) can be of great value in making tough decisions about the use and abuse of power.

Strong feelings about the use of power are, of course, rather common in the realm of changes in leadership. If leaders recognize their own ethical responses, they can adjust their behavior to be more appropriate, less damaging, and more inspiring. Eventually unfeeling, uncaring leaders find that they are bereft of self-knowledge, having little use for such things as ethics or empathy; they rarely show remorse, much less do they acknowledge their responsibility toward stockholders, employees, or the community in general. These leaders do more harm than good; honest mistakes can be forgiven and even redeemed, but callous behavior leaves destruction in its wake.

As we progress toward the 2020s and beyond, we are witnessing substantial abuses of power in a number of leadership situations in the US and around the world. These abuses create seemingly-intractable problems for vast numbers of people and overshadow the hopes and ambitions of upcoming generations. Unless we insist that our leaders use their power in ethical ways that uphold social principles based on respect, decency, and working for the common good, we may find ourselves returning to the geopolitical and economic tensions that led to two catastrophic world wars in the 20th century.

As a rule, creative leaders whose ethical and moral priorities are firmly established can imagine the positive possibilities that are unleashed when attention to the common good is combined with the healing power of love. Such leaders typically realize that they are not all that "good"; they display humility and are able to avoid simplistic dualistic thinking *(either/or* ways of seeing the world) because they realize that all the things they do, no matter what their motivation, hold the potential of producing good or producing evil. Often it's beyond the control of the leader to be sure that what they do has a good result; taking responsibility for what goes wrong (and correcting it whenever possible) is part of responsible leadership.

Getting personal: Questions for your consideration:

1. How and why does the issue of ethics matter in leadership roles?

2. What personal experience or story could demonstrate your awareness of the importance of using power in ethical ways?

3. What emotional and mental resistance are leaders likely to have concerning the importance of ethics?

Reflection question I: What particular situation have you experienced as a leader in which ethics played a decisive role in how things were handled?

Reflection question II: How would you define ethical behavior in your line of work?

Principle VII: Cultivate a sense of humor

Gligor was from a small village far from the sophistication of a big city. He was very bright and did well in school, leading to his acceptance to the most prestigious university in his country. Gligor studied diligently and graduated with high honors. His first job in the 1980s was as an accountant in a state-run manufacturing business. Gligor reported for work and found a department in disarray. The director had just learned that he had lung cancer and was not expected to live long. All around were long faces and deep sighs, as the director was much-loved by his firm. Gligor felt the sadness in the office and decided to lift the spirits of these people whom he barely knew by telling some of the funny stories his grandmother used to share about her own childhood living on a farm. These stories were full of clever animals, snowstorms depositing mountains of snow, cunning neighbors who outsmarted themselves, and pompous landlords who always managed to step into the manure. Before long, Gligor had lightened the mood of the entire department and made the director's life a pleasure rather than a struggle with fear. He told some of these funny stories to Business Leadership Forum: USA *participants, giving all of us a break from the hard work of learning to lead.*

Humor builds relationships

Over our years of working with leaders from many different countries, industries, companies, and organizations, one key principle that we've found spanning cultures is the importance of having and using a powerful and profound sense of humor. Being able to step back from challenges and see them from a different perspective is a must for any leader who wants to be effective in the liberal democratic tradition. Leaders who understand the value of humor (seeing the comical and the ironic in everyday situations) are well-equipped to make lasting and productive alliances with people of good will. Rather than engaging in manipulative and self-serving behavior, these leaders build trust and good communication through their use of humor and a pleasant demeanor.

The key measure of real leadership can be found in how people are influenced and changed for the better by the leader's character, vision, and actions. Central to all of these attributes in having a great sense of humor. As Mark Twain put it, "Humor is the good-natured side of truth." When things are funny, people tend to relax and can better pay attention to what's happening around them, giving them a fresh mind and a way to see the opportunities hidden in their problems.

Humor helps people cope with stress and can inspire people to lofty goals. Leaders who habitually approach problems and miscommunications with well-intentioned humor (not cutting sarcasm or pessimistic cynicism) have a crucial advantage in situations where mistrust and miscommunication can lead to disaster. Humor helps leaders to show their followers how to give their best in difficult and challenging circumstances, whereas lack of humor can make for a grim and frightening scenario in situations that challenge the people and resources of an organization.

Humor that builds people up

Of course, humor must be used in timely and appropriate ways. Making fun of problems is fine; making fun of people can be hurtful. Effective leaders know the difference and honor the people around them by showing respect for each person's dignity while defusing tension with a funny remark or two. These leaders know when and how to use humor to encourage people and let them step outside the situation for a minute, to regain their sense of proportion in the face of stress.

Nowhere is the value of humor more evident than in the personal relationships that make common efforts worthwhile. Humor builds bonds and makes teamwork a means of deep satisfaction as leaders and followers share the emotions engendered by taking things in stride. Wise leaders inspire the people around them to move from the status quo into the future by maintaining their own good attitude in the face of challenges. Energy, ideas, and new levels of cooperation are created by the atmosphere of good will and optimism that humor creates.

The "Big Bang" theory in action

When we started our *Business Leadership Forum: USA* leadership development programs in the 1990s, we made a number of trips to Prague to negotiate an agreement with the Czechoslovak government as to what kind of internships, university lectures, housing, and transportation ILI would provide in the US to the executive participants, and what the government would do to support these participants before, during, and after the programs. We got to know our Czechoslovak government counterparts and established what we thought were effective communications with them. Since I speak both Czech and English and have lived in Prague and the US, it seemed we had no great areas of misunderstanding after many hours of person-to-person discussion of the terms and logistics of the programs, as well as the exchange of written proposals and amendments.

One memorable trip was made to sign the official contract for the initial *Business Leadership Forum: USA* program in Jacksonville, Florida. For this ceremonial signing, we brought officials from our strategic partner, the Jacksonville Chamber of Commerce, and several Jacksonville business leaders who had a strong interest in working with ILI program participants. When we arrived at the Czechoslovak Ministry of Industry and Trade, representatives led us to a large wood-paneled board room, bedecked with little Czechoslovak and American flags, name placards, flowers, glasses of water, and an assortment of pens. The Czechs were taking the signing very seriously; the Americans were a bit taken aback at the formal and decorous atmosphere.

As we took our seats at the long table, we heard an enormous explosive sound coming from the building's cellar. I drew on my Czech sense of humor to say in English, "Apparently we have arrived with a big bang." But no one laughed, as the Americans were uneasy at the sound, and the Czechs didn't know what I'd said. Worry and tension filled the room.

Then our translator made an "inspired" translation to the Czech officials: "Mr. Tusek says the Americans have arrived with a big bank." Still no one laughed; the Czechs took the remark seriously, and the Americans were bewildered at what was happening.

So I explained for my colleagues what the translator has said, laughing to show the humor of his misunderstanding of two words that sounded identical to his ears: "bang" and bank." My American colleagues got the joke and laughed, while the translator, with typical Czech understated humor, told the Czechs why the Americans were laughing. At once, the atmosphere in the room relaxed, and we signed the contract with more mutual understanding than we had before the "big bang" explosion. (We later learned that the sound was a gas explosion in the cellar; fortunately, no major damage was done.)

Don't take yourself too seriously

These somewhat complicated negotiations paved the way for a good relationship between ILI and the Ministry of Industry and Trade, contributing to the success of the *Business Leadership Forum: USA* programs. It became clear to me from the "big bang/bank" incident that humor, used at the right time, can bring people together in a way that nothing else can. We saw how people with vastly different backgrounds, life experiences, and expectations can have their spirits elevated and draw closer as humans through humor. The small joke I told became a means of showing each other our similarities, which are at least as powerful as our differences.

In the relationships we made during our years of running the *Business Leadership Forum: USA* programs for leaders from Croatia, Lithuania, Macedonia, Romania, Bulgaria, and the Czech and Slovak Republics, we came to realize that younger leaders are not at all responsive to the dry atmosphere and lack of humor found in the old, bureaucratic institutions that prevailed under the Central and Eastern European state-planned economies of the latter half of the 20th century. These younger leaders would agree that laughter is essential for productive working relations: it reduces the social distance between people, promotes teamwork, sparks productivity, and is good for personal health.

Leadership is a serious task, both an honor and an obligation. It can be tempting to see yourself and your decisions as so vital, so crucial, that you become a kind of national treasure. From there, it's a short path to becoming pompous and self-important, then on to becoming a dictatorial petty tyrant whose word is law.

Humor and humility seem to go hand-in-hand, providing a counterbalance to excessive conceit and unrealistic self-reliance. When we can see our own mistakes and failures not as deadly errors but as regrettably human folly, we are better able to accept our own limitations. This can lead to humility and a more realistic sense of self, both of which are a good antidote to the tendency that leaders develop to see themselves as operating on a higher plane than other people. From the discussion of misuse of power in the preceding chapter (*Use your power in ethical ways*), we know that leaders can forget that they are not perfect. They can become dictatorial and short-sighted, using their power only for their own benefit. The ability to find yourself amusing is tied to maintaining a sense of proportion as to your own abilities. Pride is brought down by laughing at its foolishness.

Humor that heals

In terms of health benefits, well-publicized reports from such influential organizations as the Mayo Clinic indicate that laughter stimulates the heart, helps move air through the lungs, and increases blood circulation. In the same way that aerobic exercise aids in the development of endorphins (the "feel-good" hormones), laughter can facilitate the release of endorphins and other beneficial hormones. Laughter can strengthen the immune system by alleviating chronic stress and can even relieve pain. There are no adverse effects from laughter that we know of, so why not have a good laugh every day?

We recall an instance in our *Business Leadership Forum: USA* programs that illustrates the healing power of humor. One of our participants from Central Europe, a young executive named Darina, came down with a cold that she couldn't shake off. She didn't seem to be enjoying her time in the US and was showing obvious signs of homesickness and depression. We weren't sure how to approach her but noticed that she was friendly with Gligor, the participant who was famous for his sense of humor. So we talked to Gligor in private to see what could be done to help Darina.

Gligor said, "How about a nice dinner by the ocean?" We agreed and took Gligor and Darina out to a very nice restaurant on the beach the next evening. We had a great time together, telling funny stories about our experiences and sharing jokes. Darina began to cheer up as we showed her she was not isolated, alone, and far from home—she had friends who enjoyed her company and wanted to share a relaxing evening with her.

After that dinner, Darina got more enthusiastic about her program activities and business seminars. She spent more time with the other participants and joined them for social events. She returned to the beach to get fresh air and exercise, which further lifted her spirits. The cold that had lingered went away, and Darina was able to fully take part in all the opportunities around her.

The dinner with Gligor was the key to her adjustment to strange circumstances. He persuaded her not to build a monument to her suffering and sadness, but to take a step back and see things differently. All it took were some amusing stories and a few good jokes for Darina to relax and make the most of what was, for her, a very challenging program. Humor heals, and no leader can afford to ignore such an accessible source of good health.

The hallmark of leadership: a sense of proportion

Humor invites us to see ourselves as well-equipped to lead, but also as flawed and capable of error. Learning to put our own mistakes in a humorous light helps us to see how our actions and decisions as a leader don't operate in a vacuum. We may have the best ideas and intentions, but changing circumstances around us can distort and even negate our plans, leading to consequences ranging from the inconvenient to the tragic.

Humor may not be the first, best reaction to true disaster, but it may help alleviate some feelings of desperation and the frozen reaction of being at the end of your rope. Try a small bit of humor, even if you share it with no one but yourself. It may be enough to propel you into new ways of coping and recovering. Try to find the humor, the incongruity, and the surprise in every situation.

Great leaders, those who are worth emulating, find ways to incorporate humor and a cheerful frame of mind into their own attitudes. They create an atmosphere that is the opposite of forbidding and threatening by emphasizing what's light-hearted and positive. With such a mindset, problems become less overwhelming; a joke and a kind word give people a break from anxiety and bring a new perspective in which what's wrong becomes the pathway to what's right.

Those fortunate leaders who can discern who they are and find ways to express that with a sense of humor can inspire others to create a different future. Keeping a sense of proportion—a sense of humor—is a key element in the role of leadership. When humor shapes the leader's day-to-day behavior (rather than trying to use humor only in scripted, forced-seeming social events), that leader is seen as authentic and trustworthy. Such behavior proves especially helpful in times of significant change, when people are likely to drag their feet and need reinforcement to continue to move forward. The leader's sense of humor makes all the difference.

While leaders come in all shapes and sizes, most leaders in advanced democracies have a well-developed sense of humor. They rely on humor to keep their egos in check, their feet on the ground, and their relationships cordial. Humor relieves tension and builds trust; even the worst piece of news is not so unbearable when the team can share some levity. Humor motivates people by reducing anxiety and disarming those who would rain down despair and gloom in trying circumstances. Humor heals the body and the mind; it soothes the soul and spirit.

In many ways, the sole measure of real leadership is how people react to the leader's character, vision, and actions. A well-developed sense of humor can bring it all together for the leader who cares enough to explore every means of leading with purpose. Leadership is far too important to be taken too seriously; humor is the last great refuge of truth and human contact.

Getting personal: Questions for your consideration:

1. What is humor, in your own terms? Give an example of a time when you used humor to lessen tension and encourage the people you lead.

2. Would you rather drive people to achieve organizational goals or create a relaxed and pleasant atmosphere in which to work?

3. What are the intrinsically valuable and tangible benefits of cultivating a sense of humor?

Reflection question I: *Recall a time when you used humor to defuse an explosive situation or turn around a particularly challenging set of circumstances. Where did you find the inspiration for your humor?*

Reflection question II: *How can you be confident that your humor is "translating" well to the people you lead who are from different social and cultural backgrounds? List a few inoffensive ways to use humor in your job.*

Afterword: The changes don't stop

In the seven principles of leadership in this leadership primer, I have summarized the key observations that we pinpointed from witnessing, and to a certain degree participating in, the changes in leadership in Croatia, Lithuania, Macedonia, Romania, Bulgaria, and the Czech and Slovak Republics during the decades after the fall of state-planned communism from the late 1980s to the 2000s.

My hope has been to present principles that can serve as inspiration for the leaders of tomorrow, and at the same time, to capture (at least to a degree) that peculiar period of time right after 1989 when long-slumbering dreams were awakened in Central and Eastern Europe. These dreams, plans, and wishes for a better economy, more personal freedom, a greater voice in politics, a more free and open society, and a more enjoyable life have so far only partly materialized as the world has been changing in ways that were impossible to predict.

Aftershocks of unexpected change

The aftershocks of 1989's rapid successive toppling of communist regimes in Central and Eastern Europe did not abate overnight. As people and organizations grabbed for whatever power seemed to be temporarily unguarded, confusion and working at cross-purposes became the order of the day in many of these post-communist countries. But regardless of whether the revolution was "velvet," as in Czechoslovakia, or bloody, as in the former Yugoslavia, it became clear that the post-WWII era was finally at an end.

As the old totalitarian regimes receded into irrelevance, political and economic earthquakes threatened to shake the formerly frozen topography of the Soviet bloc. Events moved quickly as a new, united Europe was born. Yet from the start, the transition to the new Europe was marked by distortions in the transfer of economic and political power. In Central and Eastern Europe, the privatization process for businesses, the establishment of free and open elections, the giving back of state-confiscated properties to individual owners, the curriculum changes in state-run educational institutions, and the re-negotiation procedures between church and state (which had taken over church properties and interfered with church policies) were areas ripe for corruption, misunderstanding, and plain incompetence. Strong, just leadership was essential, but where would those leaders come from?

The European Union promised a united Europe, one that bound nations together with trade and open borders that let citizens of quite different countries mix freely. With the opening of the former Soviet bloc to trade, the potential was there to remake Europe into a quasi-federation (with minimal legal and military obligations) that could rival the US in economic power and prestige. But right from the start, illegalities and shady dealings marred the privatization process for former state-owned companies.

The lack of engagement and involvement by nations in Western Europe in this process, while understandable in terms of national sovereignty, made it too easy for slick operators from all over the world to grab the most valuable assets of countries whose communist past left them vulnerable to capitalist strategies that were unknown and often skirted the edges of legality, not to mention ethics and morality. There was no US-sponsored "Marshall Plan" oversight to organize funding and controls on the markets in these newly open nations, and criminal elements were quick to move in.

ILI and Czechoslovakia

This is not to say that all business was corrupt or questionable in terms of ethics. For example, in Czechoslovakia, respectable German and Dutch firms were among the earliest investors and buyers of venerable manufacturers such as Skoda automobiles. But even though many business transactions were legally performed, the fact remained that much of the wealth of the former Communist nations was being snapped up by foreigners and by former Communist leaders using money stashed abroad or borrowed from organized crime.

And this is precisely where the International Leadership Institute saw a once-in-a-lifetime opportunity to make a major contribution to shoring up the fledgling non-communist governments of Central and Eastern Europe, starting with Czechoslovakia. We wanted to be part of the changeover from a state-planned economy to an open, competitive market; we knew this changeover could be best accomplished with help from those who were already doing it. In other words, we saw the chance to connect executives from the top Czechoslovak companies with American firms that could show, not just tell, how to compete in the global economy, based on their relatively successful experience in international business.

If you were to compare the economic and political transformation from communism to democracy and capitalism in the countries of the former Soviet bloc in the early 1990s, you might note that East Germany was leading the pack. This was due to tremendous help (in funding, reestablishment of political institutions, and overall encouragement) from West Germany; the two countries reunited in October 1990. Poland, Hungary, Romania, and

Czechoslovakia were not so fast in recovering from their decades of communist one-party rule and closed markets. Although totalitarianism as a leadership philosophy was officially over, the people occupying positions of leadership did not change overnight.

The Czechs, for example, had many of these old-style bureaucrats, or "structures," still in power. It would perhaps be too much to expect that all of these leaders would immediately and voluntarily cast aside their longstanding assumptions about the most desirable or appropriate leadership principles and practices. Their past performance and career accomplishments, once praised and rewarded, were being called into question and challenged; it's not surprising that many reacted defensively, digging in their heels and refusing to change.

Trying to persuade people that change is good

From 1991-1996, in our *Business Leadership Forum: USA* programs, we first worked directly with the Ministry of Industry of Czechoslovakia and after 1993 with the Ministry of Industry and Trade of the Czech Republic. These government ministries identified the executives whom they deemed crucial for the success of the transfer from a state-run, planned, closed economy to a private, free-market, open economy and presented them to the International Leadership Institute as preferred program participants. ILI officers and program partners (from US Chambers of Commerce, businesses, universities, and volunteer host families) interviewed these pre-selected participants to gauge their English-language skills, professional abilities, organizational needs, and personal attitudes toward the on-going political and economic transformation.

This was a delicate process. Those leaders who had enjoyed positions of responsibility, privilege, and respect were suddenly confronted with a brand-new standard of success. Rather than being able to rely on the unquestioned power from which they had operated (power derived from the totalitarian communist government, which tried to control every aspect of its citizens' lives), these leaders had to develop their own personal authority based on an entirely different set of leadership principles and practices that they saw in action in the US.

In university business classes, they could see different (and, as they were repeatedly told, "better") ways of managing the people they employed, distributing the goods their factories produced, planning for the development and marketing of products, maintaining control of finances, advertising their products and services, paying their taxes, and establishing communications with suppliers, employees, customers, government agencies, and competitors.

It's not difficult to imagine the challenges these leading executives faced. Many of them, in the early days of the program, were older men whose authority had rarely been put to the test. They could point to years of successful performance in their roles and, in many cases, were either bewildered or resentful that the rug had been pulled from under their feet. Not only were they being told to change, but in what ways, exactly, they were to change was not clear.

University professors talked with these leaders about the need to restructure their business practices, emphasizing the role of executives as visionary decision-makers. Host families showed them entirely different ways to spend leisure time, buy the necessities and luxuries of life, act as responsible community members and citizens, worship God (in some families), and relate to friends and family members, including children. Internship sponsors in US-based businesses demonstrated how to do business in a competitive free-market economy where finding customers and selling products are the key to success (whereas under communism, simply making products was the main goal).

ILI officers urged these leaders to adapt to American customs quickly, so as to make the most of their short time in the USA. Imagine going from a position of unquestioned authority to the position of constant student—and in a foreign language! We have to admire the tenacity and determination of the great majority of our executive participants as they forged their own path in their *Business Leadership Forum: USA* programs.

Change, change, change—and quickly! But our participants weren't given simple formulas for change. In a fluid, rapidly-transforming global economy, there are no simple formulas. Each business and institution must do three things to endure, let alone succeed:

1. Articulate and live out the core values, principles, and

vision that all agree on.

2. Communicate with all stakeholders (customers, clients, employees, owners, community) with a consistent message that inspires them to create a different and better future.

3. Be alert for new opportunities and be able to change quickly when needed.

Technology, social change, and the uncertain future

Adding to the mix of personal and professional change is the development of technologies that have radically changed the landscape of international business. In the early 90s, the world-wide web, email, and social media were pushing aside such old-time communication methods as telephone and fax (and Czechoslovakia was not well-supplied with either, in any case!). The successful executive must be tech-savvy, or hire those who are. For leaders who were used to top-down communication, these horizontal ways of making decisions were, no doubt, quite threatening.

Needless to say, not every ILI executive participant welcomed all these challenges; not every participant was easy to work with or grateful (at the time) for the opportunity to revamp his or her entire professional life. Yet for us, the ongoing change and pressing need for authentic leadership added a sense of urgency to our task of equipping leaders with the new skills and attitudes they needed in order to survive in the global economy. We were prepared to work with our participants, regardless of their attitudes and preconceptions.

ILI persisted in offering the *Business Leadership Forum: USA* programs. We had such positive feedback from our strategic partners in government agencies such as the Czechoslovak Ministry of Industry and Trade and the US Department of State; non-profit organizations including more than a dozen Chambers of Commerce and universities in Europe and the US; more than 900 businesses in the US and Europe; and the generous people who hosted our program participants for so many social and cultural events that we knew the programs were valuable and important.

Our partners had many different motivations for being involved in the political and economic transformations of the former Soviet bloc. Why would Americans care about the fate of people living in small, far-away countries?

1. Some of our most enthusiastic American partners and supporters were looking for business opportunities in emerging markets to "lubricate the wheels of progress" and were able to forge relationships that still endure.

2. Many host families wanted to extend the hand of friendship and have kept in touch with the executives they hosted.

3. University professors sought opportunities for academic exchanges with people from Central and Eastern European countries to enrich their understanding of economic and political development on a global scale.

We worked with the Czech government until 1996, when Prime Minister Vaclav Klaus declared that the Czech transition was complete, and his government would not continue programs aimed at assisting in that historic change.

For the next decade, ILI worked with the US Department of State, Agency for International Development, in its AID programs for Eastern European countries in transition from communism. We hosted AID programs for leaders from Macedonia, Bulgaria, Croatia, Romania, Lithuania, and Slovakia, helping participants from a spectrum of industries and professions to break into international markets and develop their countries' infrastructures.

Post 9/11 (September 11, 2001), the attack on the US that startled the world, international business and politics have changed in fundamental ways. Fears of terrorism and the rise of religious fundamentalist militancy have inflamed ancient prejudices and created a "fortress" mentality that encourages hatred and isolationism. While some nations are choosing to close their borders, build walls, limit immigration, and withdraw from international cooperation, the clear path for the future is more, not less, commerce among the countries of the world.

In fact, we at ILI have great faith that leaders will arise to overcome the current spirit of division and suspicion. We have dedicated our professional lives to assisting people in developing their leadership skills, and we have seen again and again that leaders are not only born, but are made, when people decide to lead whole-heartedly and respond to the challenge of being authentic, trustworthy, and morally-responsible agents of change.

We believe that the seven basic leadership principles that have been the core of our leadership development programs since 1985 resonate across cultures, across borders, and across time. Leading is never easy, but sound advice and lessons learned can help us all.

We hope this handbook on leadership will provide you, the reader, with a reliable, respectable blueprint to enable you to become engaged and to be inspired to fully commit to being effective in all your leadership roles, both now and in years to come. If you have found *Leaders to Follow: A Leadership Handbook for the 21st Century* to be valuable in these times of dramatic changes in the economic, political, and social fabric of the world, we would love to hear from you.

--Jaroslav B. Tusek, 2018

Winter Springs, Florida.

References: A short list of publications on leadership

Capital in the Twenty-First Century, Thomas Piketty, Belknap Press: An Imprint of Harvard University Press, reprint edition, 2017.

Control Your Destiny or Someone Else Will, Noel Tichy and Stratford Sherman, Harper Business, reprint edition, 2005.

"Hubris syndrome: An acquired personality disorder? A study of US Presidents and UK Prime Ministers over the last 100 years," David Owen and Jonathan Davidson, *Brain*, Volume 132, Issue 5, 1 May 2009.

Prague for Beginners: Finding Myself in Prague, Sara Tusek, International Leadership Institute Publications, 2017.

Saving Capitalism: For the Many, Not the Few, Robert Reich, Vintage, reprint edition, 2016.

Slovakia on the Road to Independence, Paul Hacker, Penn State University Press, 1st edition, 2011.

The End of Leadership, Barbara Kellerman, Harper Business, first edition, 2012.

The End of Work: The Decline of the Global Labor Force and the Dawn of the Post-Market Era, Jeremy Rifkin, Tarcher, first edition, 1994.

The M Form Society: How American Teamwork Can Recapture the Competitive Edge, William Ouchi, Addison-Wesley Publishing Company, 1984.

The Mighty and the Almighty: Reflections on America, God, and World Affairs, Madeleine Albright, Harper Perennial, 2007.

"The Tragedy of Central Europe," Milan Kundera, translated by Edmund White, *New York Review of Books*, Volume 31, Number 7, April 26, 1984.

21st Century Jobs, Jaroslav B. Tusek and Sara Tusek, International Leadership Institute Publications, 2nd edition, 2018.

Appendix I: Comments and insights from ILI program participants

"On behalf of the Ministry of Industry and Trade of the Czech Republic, I should like to thank you for the possibility that is given to Czech managers through the Executive Education program. This program is highly appreciated by the Ministry not only for its significant contribution in the field of extremely high level of knowledge which is offered to the participants but also for the business opportunities which are arising from the internship part of the program."

--Radomír Sabela, Deputy Minister, Ministry of Industry and Trade of the Czech Republic, 1993

"Twenty-five years ago we were just returning from our stay in Chattanooga. The whole program was an unbelievable experience for us. It represented an amazing possibility in our career and professional development, as well as a chance to learn about the USA. Thank you again, after all these years, for having such a wonderful idea and making it into reality.

My career has been rather successful. After earning an MBA from the Rochester Institute of Technology, I worked for the European Bank for Reconstruction and Development for 18 years; for six of these years, I lived and worked in London. Right now I am planning another trip to the US for Fall 2018—this time I want to visit major US national parks in the West."

—Zdenka Vicarova, 2018

"I participated in an International Leadership Institute program in summer 1996. This summer of 2016 will already be 20 years since I had taken the program, but I can say that I still profit from this experience. The rich program which was provided to us gave us insight into different areas. *What participation in the program brought to me in particular:*

- Improvement of language skills, which then made my University studies easier. At the time when I started to study at Charles University in Prague, there was little teaching material for my major, Japanese studies, written in the Czech language. Almost everything was in English; therefore, my English knowledge was a big benefit.

- It was a very good experience and awakened in me the desire to learn more about the world in the future. It helped me to adapt easily to new surroundings and people later on, during my years of living and working in Japan.

My program taught me how to find my own goal and pursue it. I never forget Sara's and Jarda's words: everything is possible, and there is no word '*but*'. I understood that interest and enthusiasm are half of the journey to success. If there is a will, there is a way!"

--Sylvie Brandejsova, 2016

"I think you tackle the leadership issue well from the perspective of someone who helped shaped the (almost) first generation of democratic leaders in the Czech Republic.

In the argument that "everyone is born a leader," good leaders are above all defined by good followers, so it is perfectly fine to be a follower; it comes with no pejorative inferiority stigma. Neither does it mean that leadership excludes followers: leader and follower both form leadership - at least in my humble opinion.

I was thinking . . . how millennials think about work and how this generation will no longer abide by the rules of '20th century leadership'. Millennials are no longer willing to abide by the 9/5 money-chasing environment. We are not afraid to quit a job if we are trampled on by our bosses, and it is mostly a good working environment and collective that will attract us."

--Marketa Bajgeriova, 2017

"I can't believe it was just a year ago I was finishing my stay in the United States. I remember it as vividly as if it were yesterday. I saw so many interesting places and met a lot of nice people. . . I have spent this year in new conditions and a new environment for me. I was looking for new customers, preparing materials—starting my new job as a consultant. Thank you again for your care and all that you have done for me."

--Miroslav Grecny, 1995

Dear Sara, dear Jarda,

Nice to hear from you! As I wrote to Sara, I cannot wait to read your new book! I'm so happy that you are coming to Prague; it will be lovely to meet again.

My experience from taking a course at ILI:

I took part in the leadership development course at a turning point in my career, finishing one job at an architecture firm and starting at another one (was it in 2012?). It was an opportunity for me to start thinking about what I really want to do professionally. I had been for a long time in "auto-pilot" mode, quite happy but not doing things so intentionally and intensely. Though I realized that I'm the only one who can answer to the question "what's my calling," it was really helpful to be part of a group and reflect on this together.

Two exercises were meaningful to me. The first one was to think about my values. This was great to discern what type of work/projects/companies I want to do and to work with, without compromise. The second exercise was about listing our achievements. I appreciated that, as it highlighted past experiences to build upon. I could see that even though my career had been short, it was already full with many interesting projects, both at work and outside. It helped to build self-confidence, and to this day I still keep a record of realizations.

Since taking the course I've reoriented myself more towards design education. This provides me with more flexibility and satisfaction. And the free time I gained is reinvested in my family and development of self-initiated creative projects.

Lots of love,

--Marie Doucet, 2016

"After more than six months I still have very big impressions from my stay in the US. I use the experiences every day.

In the beginning of this year, Bob Frederick and his wife (from my internship at TC Lumber Company) visited our country, our business, and my family for several days. The Ahlstrom people (my other internship sponsor) visit me very often. I try to help them here, and we prepare a trade cooperation between us.

In case you come to Prague, I would be very pleased to meet with you both. I can help you with new activity in our country."

--Jaroslav Libal, 1993

"My positive evaluation has not changed. There is no doubt; it was a great chance for me to participate in the *Business Leadership Forum: USA* program, and I want to thank you for choosing me. I gained many experiences there that are very useful to me.

I knew it would not be easy for me to apply my new knowledge in such a giant company as Komerční banka. I have an excellent job offer in Prague . . . I was interviewed by Ellen Hayes from Personnel Select and she could offer me very interesting possibilities. By the way, she knows you, which was a very big surprise for me. I hope there will be another chance of meeting you here soon."

--Mirka   Jakubova,   1994

"Hi, you-all, who have had an opportunity to read this publication, published by Jarda and Sara and their team. When I was asked to contribute my own comments to this publication about our Executive Education program in the US, in which (together with my colleagues) I participated in 1992, I did not hesitate to respond. I'd like to write down at least a few memories and share with others my personal view of our stay in the US. It's my way to thank all those people who made our stay possible.

Overview: Our group of twelve executives was the pilot group of the *Business Leadership Forum: USA* programs organized by the International Leadership Institute and (at that time) the Czechoslovak Ministry of Industry and Trade. This pilot program gave us the opportunity to visit the US and learn as much as possible about the basic principles of a market economy. It also gave us the opportunity to contribute to a better understanding of the differences between our two nations (Czechoslovakia and the US) and to think about how to erase some of the existing divisions between East and West.

We were a diverse group of twelve participants, eleven Czechs and one Slovak (Hi, Miro, how are you doing?) executives holding different positions, including CEOs, Vice Presidents, a researcher, a government leader from a key Ministry, and a second-tier executive from a large enterprise (here I am talking about myself). All these people are called "managers" in today's Czech Republic. Because we were the pilot group, we did not have the advantage of learning from the experience of past participants. We did not know what to expect. Suddenly we were arriving at Atlanta's international airport in Georgia. We were welcomed by a small group of American program organizers who drove us to Chattanooga, Tennessee, which became our "base camp" for the next three months.

Let me first make clear that all that followed was not only about discovering differences between the principles of a functioning market economy and our former communist system in Czechoslovakia. In fact, all things concerning our program were different, including our accommodations, food, and the distances we needed to travel. All in all, we found great differences between our experience in the US as compared to our life in Czechoslovakia, from the material things available to us to the ever-present feelings of freedom, hospitality, and good will coming from the people we were meeting in the US.

Clearly, there was a plethora of new things we had to adjust to, get used to, and persuade our brains (damaged by years of totalitarianism and communism) to think positively about in the US; we also had to adjust our behavior and worldview accordingly. I think in the eyes of our American counterparts, we probably looked like an exotic bunch of guys from some other part of the world. These Americans did not seem to know much about our country, with the notable exceptions of Ivan Lendl and Vaclav Havel.

Perhaps more precisely because of that, we were able to gain considerable attention and interest from our hosts, who wanted to meet our needs and wishes, as it often happens in the case of those who are first and a bit exotic to boot. Our American hosts organized various social events at their homes and other places during our free time. These events provided us with opportunities to have a peek into the "kitchen" of life on the other side of the Atlantic.

In the beginning, before we started our internships in various companies, we were meeting mostly with people from Covenant College (faculty, staff and students) in Lookout Mountain, Georgia. Covenant College, together with the World Trade Center—Chattanooga, were important partners with the International Leadership Institute in this joint venture with the Czechoslovak Ministry of Industry and Trade in Prague and the Olomouc Training Center of MORA, MORAVIA in Olomouc. The Covenant community was a group of really wonderful people who spent a lot of valuable time with us, for which we are immensely grateful.

During our internships, each of us had an outstanding opportunity to learn something new and different in our respective fields or areas of work we found interesting. Because each participant had an internship in a different industry and company, our ability to work independently, our persistence and stamina, our motivation, and our professional and language abilities were all severely tested. This in itself was a great school of life for all of us.

It's really hard to believe what Sara and Jarda, together with all the other American partners, were able to do as they organized our program. Not only did they facilitate our pilot program, but they were able to continue and improve the *Business Leadership Forum: USA* programs for many years. In fact, they continued this program, in partnership with the US Department of State till 2006. I have to say that we were taken care of in a wonderful way, and all worked smoothly. If there was any snag in the program, the partners dealt with it and found the right solution.

I think at the time that we participants were unable to fully grasp and appreciate what all those people involved in the program were doing for us, what we really gained from the whole experience or how it influenced and changed our future lives. We came back as different people as well as different executives. As a result of our program, we became more confident about what we were doing. We had modified our worldview and therefore we were more useful in our society and our places of work. We also gained significantly by improving our English language skills, making new professional contacts, and by making new friends as well. And that seems like plenty to me—don't you think so?

Personal Viewpoint: I suppose my view of our whole stay in the US may be a bit different from some of my program colleagues, and it may also be different from the hundreds of other participants in the programs that followed our pilot project. Thanks to my being young and single, I might have had an advantage that resulted in being more easily accepted, and so I have experienced plenty of friendly, sensitive and welcoming behavior from our American hosts. I was able to gain admission into this program thanks to my fluency in English, while some more experienced potential participants lacked this important and helpful qualification.

I will always remember the rare and special moment when my colleague Miro, the only Slovak participant, and I were chosen to debate students from Covenant College. I have to admit that when I saw that huge lecture hall full of professors and students, I was so nervous that I could barely remember who I was and where I came from. But when I mentioned, as I was introducing myself, that I was the youngest in the group and the only one who was single, the whole auditorium exploded into laughter! My nervousness instantly vanished and the ice had melted.

I fully enjoyed every minute of my stay from the first to the last day. I still maintain connections with several colleagues from my group of participants. Likewise, I am in touch with my American friends, after all these years (now nearly a quarter of a century). This is fabulous, I think. My stay in the US clearly had a great impact on me, and I can feel its influence even today. Finally, I'd like to thank all of the people who made our stay in the US possible. Many special thanks to Sara and Jarda. Again, thank you."

—Viktor Vacha, 2017

"I would like to thank you for your help and promotion during my participation in the *Business Leadership Forum: USA*

"Doing Business in the US" program organized by the International Leadership Institute.

My impressions from the program surpassed my expectations. Seminars in leading Florida businesses and at the University of North Florida helped me better understand American businessmen who are eager to do business with Central Europe. I developed a new perspective on the excellent prospects of my own company for doing business in the US.

I could use immediately the great opportunities and advantages from participating in the program. American businesspeople were very helpful to my successful stay in the US. The success I found would have been impossible without the excellent seminars at the University of North Florida and other interesting meetings during the program."

-- Petr Vosmik, 1995

"Just after coming back to my country, I can properly appreciate how important my American experience has been and how I can use it in daily work. During my time in Minnesota, I visited ten companies, and I started cooperation with Innovative Consulting Services, a consulting company working according to Dr. Deming's philosophy. This company has a branch in the Czech Republic, and we have already started the hard work of establishing Total Quality in my company. It is going to be interesting and very difficult as well.

In my company I have several very good employees, and their participation in your program in Florida would be very useful to them. Please send me more details about this.

--Stan Tobola, 1993

Appendix II: About the International Leadership Institute and its programs

Overview and brief history

The International Leadership Institute operates in the Czech Republic and in Florida, offering programs, services, and publications designed to help individuals develop their leadership potential, with a focus on assisting leaders and aspiring leaders in their educational and career development. Through ILIP, the Institute's publishing house, we publish books, articles, newsletters, and business materials in support of our mission.

Since our founding in Princeton, NJ, in 1985, the *International Leadership Institute* has been working with leaders and aspiring leaders to assist them in developing and using the attitudes, knowledge, and skills necessary for dynamic and responsible leadership in the context of open markets and liberal democracy.

Our US-based Executive Education programs, *Business Leadership Forum: USA* for Czech and Slovak executives (1990-1997) and our professional training programs sponsored by the US. Agency for International Development of the Department of State for Eastern European leaders from Bulgaria, Croatia, Lithuania, Macedonia, and Romania (1997-2004) had a significant impact in the transition of these formerly state-controlled communist economies to open markets and political freedom. We ran these programs with a variety of strategic partners in the US and in Europe, as listed in Appendix III. More than 350 European executives took part in these programs, along with more than 900 businesses in the US and Europe. The programs were supported by thousands of volunteers in the US and in Europe, including host families, lecturers at universities and businesses, members and officers from civic organizations, government officials, journalists, and friends.

Since 1990, we have offered the *American English Language Immersion Programs in the United States.* These programs are aimed at young Europeans, to help them develop their English language skills while learning about the social, historical, spiritual, and cultural contexts currently in place in the US. Also included in these programs is career development assistance to help participants envision their life's work and set goals in educational and professional organizations. More than 200 people have taken part in these language and career development programs, along with their host families, university lecturers, and community supporters.

2018 Vision, Mission, and Major Goals

ILI Vision

ILI will continue to engage in a discourse about what it means to be a constructive, responsible, and effective leader in the context of a liberal democratic society. ILI will promote and encourage the concept of leadership development that emphasizes the necessity for leaders to correctly evaluate (through their intimate and meaningful involvement) the strengths and weaknesses, morals and ethics, and cultural values of the communities they lead.

ILI Mission

To this end, ILI will focus on two strategies for promoting responsible leadership development:

1. ILI will organize and deliver seminars and discussions with people interested in exploring the key principles of leadership and in developing and using their own leadership potential.

2. Through ILIP (the publishing house of the International Leadership Institute), ILI will publish and promote books, articles, and program materials that inspire people to contribute their best as leaders in the communities where they live and work.

ILI Major Goals

- To publish and market *Leaders to Follow: a Leadership Handbook for the 21st Century* by Jaroslav Tusek, ILI President & CEO. This handbook, published by ILIP as an e-book and a print book, will include comments and insights from ILI program participants over the years as to how they have used the information and skills they obtained in their program to build their leadership skills in their careers.

- To engage in discussions and seminars on leadership with business executives, professional leaders, and students aspiring to leadership positions. These discussions and seminars will take place in Europe and the US.

- To publish and market the second edition of *21ˢᵗ Century Jobs* (ILIP, first edition, 2009). Sara Tusek will take the lead in this effort.

- To maintain professional relationships (especially with past participants in ILI programs) in Europe and the US, with the goal of strengthening ILI's ability to deliver relevant seminars and publications on leadership in the 21st century.

Appendix III: Selected list of ILI Strategic Partners, 1991-2007

In Czechoslovakia/Czech Republic:

Ministry of Industry and Trade of Czechoslovakia (1990-1992)

Ministry of Industry and Trade of the Czech Republic (1993-1996)

Olomouc Training Center, MORA/MORAVIA

In Florida:

Jacksonville Chamber of Commerce

Jacksonville University

Sarasota Chamber of Commerce

Stetson University, Deland

Tannenbaum SCRO, P.L., Sarasota

University of North Florida

In Georgia:

Covenant College, Lookout Mountain

In Slovakia:

Slovak Chamber of Commerce and Industry in Bratislava - Slovakia

In Tennessee:

World Trade Center—Chattanooga

In Washington, DC:

World Learning

The Department of State and US Agency for International Development (USAID)

About the Author: Jaroslav B. Tusek

In conjunction with the 33rd anniversary of the
International Leadership Institute, in *Leaders to Follow: a
Leadership Handbook for the 21st Century*, ILI President & CEO
Jaroslav B. Tusek reflects on his personal experiences with
Business Leadership Forum: USA program participants as he sets
forth the enduring principles he has gleaned from working
with executives from Europe and the US in pursuit of
leadership development.

After the collapse of communist governments in Central
and Eastern Europe in 1989 and the early 1990s, Jarda had a
vision of helping those countries in their transition from
state-planned, closed economic and political systems to open
markets operating in the context of the liberal democratic
tradition. He believed that putting time, energy, and personal

will into such a vision, along with faith, hope, and love, could bring about wonderful achievements. The *Business Leadership Forum: USA* programs exemplify how people working together towards this vision can do great things.

In his years of working with and studying internationally under leaders from academia, business, and the non-profit world—in Prague, Oslo, Geneva, Cambridge, San Francisco, New York City, and Florida—Jarda has gained a broad experience of leadership styles, theories, and principles. His tenure at the American Management Association, where he directed the Operation Enterprise program for young leaders, as well as his experiences running ILI's *Business Leadership Forum: USA*, have helped Jarda appreciate the complexities of working both cross-generationally and cross-culturally.

Jarda holds a Master's degree from Columbia University's School of International and Public Affairs. He studied at the Faculty of Law at Charles University in Prague and was a research fellow at the Peace Research Institute Oslo. He has spoken and taught at such institutions as Columbia University, St Lawrence University, the University of Oslo, and Princeton University. Jarda has published articles, commentaries, and books, as well as run seminars and workshops, on topics in international affairs, career development, and leadership principles and practices. This is his tenth book on leadership and career development topics. Jarda has been married to Sara Tusek, ILI Managing Director, since 1995. They have two children and one grandchild living in Syracuse and New York City.

Joe kind
copied lawyer
Pod.

Fuller to my notes
email for also now...

take out of the trust to pay
tax ~~owed by my father~~
~~in circums~~ arising from
actions taken unilaterally
by my father. ~~Furthermore~~
~~my sisters I have asked~~
~~that our father stop taking~~
~~funds from the trust, yet~~
~~he continues to take income from~~
~~the trust without the our consent.~~
~~we ask that this stops as~~
~~we are the majority trustees.~~

Made in United States
Orlando, FL
06 July 2024

48637767R00104